# THORNEY
# LONDON'S
# FORGOTTEN ISLAND

## THE DENSEST CONCENTRATION OF "HISTORY" IN EUROPE

First published in 2025
by Shakespearesmonkey
174 Ashley Gardens
London SW1P 1PD

ISBN:  978-0-9540762-9-0

Cover Illustration & Design by Christopher Keegan
www.chriskeegan.co.uk

Editing & Formatting by The Amethyst Angel

Victor Keegan's blogs:
OnLondon.co.uk (Lost London section)
LondonMyLondon.co.uk
victorkeegan.com
Instagram - vickeegan
Flickr - Flickr.com/shakespearesmonkey
X(Twitter): @vickeegan
@BritishWino
@LonStreetwalker
@ShakespearesLon
@Twoems

Contact: victor.keegan@gmail.com

First Edition

# CONTENTS

# Other books by Victor Keegan

**Non-Fiction:**

Lost London (1)

Lost London (2)

**Poetry:**

Crossing the Why

Big Bang

Remember to Forget

Alchemy of Age

London my London

Selective Memories

Duelling Poets (with Michelle Gordon)

# Introduction

For my two previous books on Lost London I was able to choose from the whole of central London. To go from that vast expanse to the small acreage of Thorney Island proved a bigger challenge than I was expecting, even though it is within walking distance of my own home. This was because of the huge amount of buried history in such a small space with events and people often overlapping with each other.

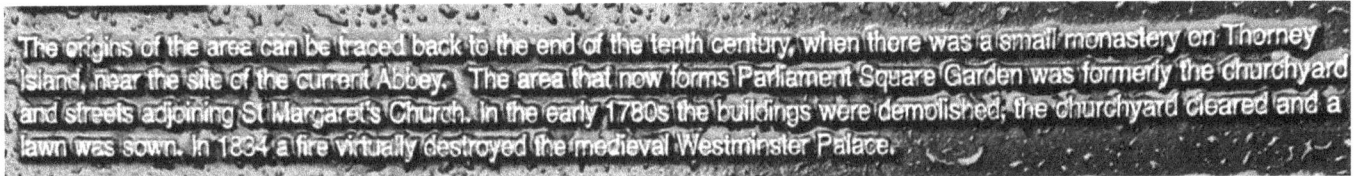

The origins of the area can be traced back to the end of the tenth century, when there was a small monastery on Thorney Island, near the site of the current Abbey. The area that now forms Parliament Square Garden was formerly the churchyard and streets adjoining St Margaret's Church. In the early 1780s the buildings were demolished, the churchyard cleared and a lawn was sown. In 1834 a fire virtually destroyed the medieval Westminster Palace.

An explanation on a metallic notice board in Parliament Square outside St Margaret's Church introduces the name "Thorney Island" for those with good sight. It is the only public recognition of the name I have come across. It states at the beginning: "The origins of the area can be traced back to the end of the tenth century, when there was a small monastery on Thorney Island, near the site of the present Abbey".

The view from the notice board is the fading green grass of Parliament Square which was once the churchyard of St Margaret's and its surrounding streets, until the streets were demolished in the 1780s. This was not very long after 1750 when the narrow Lindsay Lane (later called Dirty Lane), an historic link between Old Palace Yard and Millbank since at least 1593, was destroyed to make way for "improvements" associated with the new Westminster Bridge. This blasted a busy road between Westminster Abbey on one side and the Palace of Westminster on the other, thereby depriving the future World Heritage site of the unity of being in one uninterrupted place.

There are only two books that I know of that include the word "Thorney" in the title. One is *The Gem of Thorney Island* by the Rev James Ridgway, written in 1860. The other is the wonderfully detailed publication of the Museum of London, *The royal palace and town of Westminster on Thorney Island* based on archaeological excavations between 1991-98 for the Jubilee Line extension project.

As with my other books, this one was researched, photographed and written with my mobile phone and iPad. The popularity of AI search engines will obviously change how books are written in the future. At present they are promising a bit more than they can deliver, but I was impressed enough to use an AI generated graphic for the chapter on George IV's escape from his own Coronation banquet almost at the end of the book.

This is very much a journalist's book following avenues that took my fancy rather than a historical narrative. I hope you will enjoy.

*Vic Keegan*

# 1: Preface

Years ago, when working for the Guardian, I would occasionally take a short cut along a thoroughfare in Westminster called Old Pye Street. On the side of the road on the corner of St Ann's Lane there was a tiny building that was home to an outfit called The Thorney Island Society (and Friends of St James's and the Green Park). I presumed it to be a pleasantly eccentric organisation as I knew of no islands nearby apart from the one I was standing on formed by England, Scotland and Wales.

It was only after retirement that I stopped to read what it was all about. It turned out there was, and indeed still is, an island in the centre of London. Formed, it is claimed, by the junction of the Tyburn river - now running underground in the sewage system - with the Thames.

Thorney Island has history on its side. It is the site of a former monastery, Westminster Abbey, the two Houses of Parliament, Westminster School and until the fire of 1834, nearly all of the major law courts before they moved to the Strand, not to mention the predecessor of Big Ben. For 500 years it was also the site of the main Royal Palace from where England and sometimes Britain was ruled. Some of the remains are still on view.

Most of Thorney Island is covered by buildings and a road that runs from Parliament Square to Millbank. This means that you can't walk anywhere on these few acres without treading on the actual footsteps of the famous and the infamous, from Oliver Cromwell to William Shakespeare and also the most powerful and the most weak. It is surely the densest concentration of "history" in such a small area to be found anywhere - yet hardly anyone knows about it including many of those who work there.

For much of its existence, the walled perimeter of the core of Thorney Island protected its rich inhabitants and its sheltered monks from the harsh realities of life. Barely a hundred yards away was what Charles Dickens popularised as "The Devil's Acre" in the first edition of his weekly magazine, Household Words. It was arguably the most socially deprived and morally degraded area in the whole of Britain.

Archaeologists and historians are still debating the exact course of the Tyburn and the extent to which Thorney Island was formed by the Tyburn (now flowing in a sewer under Great College Street) and the Thames, or whether Thorney was just a tidal island in the Thames. Either way, there is no doubt that it existed even though it is little known.

Little known? When I eventually joined the Thorney Island Society, I was pleasantly surprised to be able to visit buildings in the area to which the Society was given access, but which normally were difficult for members of the public to gain entry to. On one such occasion we were taken through the Houses of Parliament to see the private rooms of the Speaker. Halfway through, our leader - an official House of Commons guide - took me aside and whispered: "Excuse me for asking, but where exactly is Thorney Island?" I didn't say a word but just pointed downwards with my finger.

Old Pye Street, named after Sir Robert Pye, a crony of Oliver Cromwell) was the epicentre of the Devil's Acre. The concept of Fagin's Den in Dickens's Oliver Twist is almost certainly based on an actual school for pickpockets located in a pub called The One Tun in Perkins Rents off Old Pye Street. That school was eventually reformed by philanthropists who moved it to the building where the Thorney Island's small Archive is today. There is a plaque behind the building to commemorate this fact.

On the other side of the tiny lane is the flourishing St Andrew's Club which claims to be the oldest youth club in the world. It is on the site of a house where Henry Purcell, the great composer, was raised and in the same street where Robert "Gather ye rosebuds while ye may" Herrick also lived. It is difficult to move anywhere in this area without treading on history.

The Thorney Island Society was formed by a remarkable woman, June Stubbs, and her co-founder, Ann Carlton. They took on the powerful property corporation Land Securities which in 1985 was about to demolish London's oldest library in Great Smith Street and indeed the whole of one side of the street. June Stubbs won, and the building was saved though the library itself had already moved elsewhere. It is now the fashionable Cinnamon Club restaurant which has preserved the ethos of the library inside.

This book is, emphatically, not an exhaustive history of the area which has been well covered elsewhere. Westminster Abbey alone has had more books written about it than any other church. To write about the politics would take a lifetime. Inevitably, there are small duplications of people and events in such a small area. Like my previous books (Vic Keegan's Lost London (1) and (2)) this book is about the people and places that take my fancy.

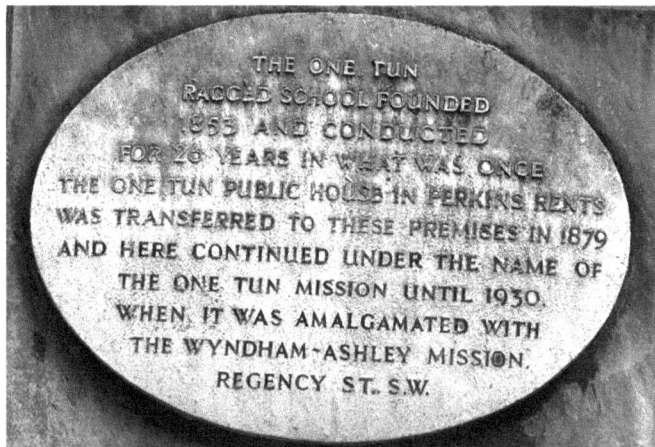

THE ONE TUN RAGGED SCHOOL FOUNDED 1853 AND CONDUCTED FOR 26 YEARS IN WHAT WAS ONCE THE ONE TUN PUBLIC HOUSE IN PERKINS RENTS WAS TRANSFERRED TO THESE PREMISES IN 1879 AND HERE CONTINUED UNDER THE NAME OF THE ONE TUN MISSION UNTIL 1930. WHEN IT WAS AMALGAMATED WITH THE WYNDHAM-ASHLEY MISSION. REGENCY ST. S.W.

# 2: Whatever happened to the River Tyburn?

What could have been a major tourist attraction for London is now buried underground - its rivers. There are four north of the Thames - the Fleet, the Westbourne, the Tyburn and the Walbrook, and two south of the river - the Effra and the Neckinger. If you want to know what they could have looked like today had they not been cemented over, then go to Wandsworth and walk the Wandle, a river once one of the most polluted in the world, but which has been restored by volunteers to become once again, at the time of writing, a chalk stream in near pristine condition.

The other rivers can't be seen, but can occasionally be heard. If you stand outside The Coach gastropub in Ray Street, Clerkenwell, you can listen to the Fleet flowing underneath the pavement from a drain. The Tyburn can be heard through one or two drains in Tachbrook Street, Victoria, but they are in the middle of the road making it hazardous to investigate. The Westbourne can't be seen except as a tubular channel running above a platform at Sloane Square underground station. The Neckinger runs underground though traces of it may be seen where it meets the Thames at St Saviour's Dock.

The actual routes of these rivers have been well established, except for one: the Tyburn. Historians and archaeologists are agreed that the first leg of its journey went from the Hampstead Hills to Buckingham Palace (albeit hidden from view by the sewer system) but thereafter the river divides… and so do the experts.

Let's take the agreed bit first. The name Tyburn derives from the Anglo Saxon word Teoburne or Teo-burna

SHEPHERD'S WELL IN 1820.

*Source of the Tyburn*

Fig 1. The Tyburn bifurcates at Buckingham Palace, one leg going to near Vauxhall Bridge and the other around Thorney Island and nearby Thorney Street

It is possible to follow the meanderings of the original Tyburn along the narrow streets of Mayfair that it flowed along. There won't be any water underneath the exact spots any more because when Sir Joseph Bazalgette constructed over 80 miles of sewers under London he had to locate them at some distance from the actual rivers so the water could be diverted when the sewers were finished.

After Mayfair, the Tyburn flows under Piccadilly - where in around 1700 at number 100 there was once a very successful "water theatre" powered by

The Chalbert bridge in Regents Park

meaning "boundary stream" or a stream separating various boundaries as the Tyburn did in the Middle Ages between the manors of Westminster and Chelsea.

It rises from a few sources including Shepherd's Well in the Hampstead Hills and flows underground in a pipe under the Chalbert bridge into Regents Park.

It carries on under Oxford Street into Mayfair. In the early 13th century the Grand Conduit was built from Oxford Street (by Bond Street) to divert much of its waters to Cheapside in the City of London which would have significantly reduced its normal flow to the Thames.

the Tyburn - and then into The Green Park, where the contours of the original river can still be discerned. The sound of the Tyburn or a tributary running along one of the sewers can be heard down a drain along one of the pathways in the photo above.

*Sounds of water under a manhole in The Green Park*

Fig 2. A view towards the south end of The Green Park showing interceptor channels.
Photo http://www.adeadendstreet.co.uk/

on the left). Its route went down Palace Street past the St James Theatre to the Cardinal Place entrance to Victoria tube station. An aerial photo taken by the constructors of the new entrance to the station (Fig 3) offers a rare example of the actual Tyburn (circled in yellow), still part of the sewer system, in full flow.

The Victoria Palace theatre is to the left and Victoria Street at the foot of the picture. When you descend into Victoria station from here you will be walking under the Tyburn.

This (Fig 2) is a glimpse of the Tyburn sewer under The Green Park looking south towards Buckingham Palace. It is a good example of the amazing brickwork still intact after more than 150 years. On the right, at least one of the connecting tunnels will be an interceptor taking surplus water - including sewage - down to treatment works in the East End.

The map (Fig 1) shows the alternative - or complementary - routes of the Tyburn from Buckingham Palace. It is generally agreed that one leg goes from Buckingham Palace to west of Vauxhall Bridge (following the arrows

Fig 3. The Tyburn (in a sewer) at Cardinal Place, Victoria Station (Constructor's photo)

It then continues across Victoria Street to flow under King's Scholar's Passage (Fig 4) to where it meets the end of Francis Street and Vauxhall Bridge Road. It is called King's Scholars' Passage because in medieval times the scholars of Westminster public school were allowed to bathe there. There won't be any opportunities to do that in future though there have been suggestions from time to time that part of it might be glassed over to reveal a bit of history.

After crossing the Vauxhall Bridge Road, the sewer then journeys under Tachbrook Street towards its historic outlet by the Thames at Grosvenor Road. There are a couple of drain holes in the middle of Tachbrook Street where what remains of the Tyburn can be heard, but as they are in the middle of an often busy street it is not advisable to do so unless you are very careful.

At the end of its trek a few hundred yards west of Vauxhall Bridge (Fig 5) there is a plaque on the river wall next to what used to be the sluice gate controlling the flow of water. These days most of the flow is diverted by interceptor channels towards treatment works in the East End but on stormy days when Bazalgette's 150

*What's left of the Tyburn river flows along Tachbrook Street to the Thames*

year old sewer system can't cope, the Tyburn empties its unforgiving flow into the Thames, sewage and all. You can still see the sluice gate keeper's house, now converted into a des-res called Tyburn House close by the exit.

This ends the undisputed course of the Tyburn from the Hampstead Hills via Buckingham Palace to near Vauxhall Bridge. The big question is did it also flow from Buckingham Palace to Old Westminster, aka Thorney Island?

This is controversial. Experts such as archaeologists

*Fig 4. King's Scholars' Passage from near Victoria Street to Vauxhall Bridge Road*

Fig 5. The sluice gate near Vauxhall Bridge where the Tyburn meets the Thames

Tim Tatton Brown and Desmond Donovan argue that the route from Buckingham Palace to Vauxhall was the natural and only course of the Tyburn and that the only way it flowed from the site of today's Buckingham Palace to Thorney Island was because there was a man-made channel in the 1080s built on the instruction of the monks of Westminster Abbey to convey water to flush out their latrines. The 1080s channel was probably used for the 13th century Abbey mill, according to Tatton Brown, but not for the later mill of 1530 which had a pond behind the "Millbank", hence the name.

This means that water from the Tyburn would have reached Thorney Island, but as a result of a diversion.

It is water from the Tyburn but not, it is argued, the traditional channel of the Tyburn itself.

Donovan argues that it is unusual for a river such as the Tyburn to divide into two branches near its mouth

A fragment of the late medieval great drain (Courtesy, Tim Tatton Brown)

and "there is no question of a delta" so an artificial channel is a likely explanation and medieval Thorney island appears to have been "an island in the tidal Thames".

This view is similar to the conclusion of the Rev James Ridgway, the author of The Gem of Thorney Island, published in 1860. He argued that Thorney Island "was formed by a small branch of the Thames which leaving that river at the end of Abingdon Street ran in a westerly direction along the line of College Street and the south side of Dean's Yard. After crossing Tothill Street it continued its course along Princes Street which until recently retained its name of Long Ditch. From there it ran in an easterly direction along Gardeners Lane, crossing King Street (today's Whitehall), Parliament Street, and Cannon Row and returned to the river near the southern extremity of the privy Gardens".

However, another group of distinguished archaeologists including Mary Nicholls, head of Environmental Archaeology at Museum of London Archaeology (MOLA), thinks otherwise. They and others have sunk numerous boreholes along the surrounding areas of Thorney Island. If you look carefully at the map of the Tyburn (Fig 1 the boreholes are represented by tiny crosses. They argue that many years ago there were deep channels that would have been a natural carrier of the waters of the Tyburn to form a delta-like formation - yes, a delta - in the broad area around Thorney Island. This would have created a number of eyots or small islands of which Thorney was likely the biggest.

They found that both the northern and southern Tyburn branches were mainly characterised by deep channels which would have been a natural route for water. Where data points (the locations of heights derived from borehole logs) are numerous – for example around Thorney Island – the model shows deep channels, between -2m and 6m - OD at the base of the channel. The reference "-6m OD" indicates that a location is 6 meters below the Ordnance Datum (OD) a UK reference point for measuring altitudes and heights based on mean sea level.

The team concludes: "Given the evident depth and definition of the channels in the lower Tyburn reach, a man-made origin for the northern branch (going to Thorney Island) seems implausible". They add that the contour plot shows the northern branch of the Tyburn splitting to encircle Thorney Island. This meant that the Tyburn on one side flowed around Thorney Island reaching the Thames by following the path of the medieval monastery wall along Great College Street (Fig 6 at the end of which it powered the monks' mill which led to the road being called Millbank.

An additional channel split off to the south to join the Thames around today's Thorney Street as can be seen in the photo (Fig 7) which shows the storm water channel, which historically, has deposited surplus storm water into the Thames when the sewers can't cope and to the right of which are the Thorney steps which give access to the foreshore subject to fast moving tides and often slippery steps. Lambeth Bridge is in the background.

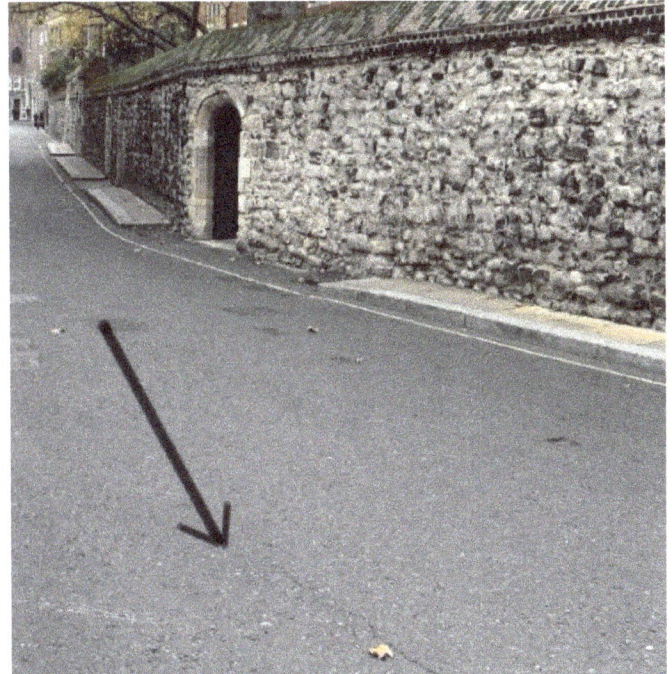

Fig 6. The Tyburn's possible route to the Thames under Great College Street

Who is right? This debate seems bound to go and on between archaeologists who have established the existence of a channel made by the monks and the painstakingly researched MOLA conclusion that the flow of the Tyburn in deep channels had a Delta effect creating a number of eyots including Thorney Island which survived to become part of a UNESCO World Heritage site at Westminster. It is possible they are both right as the authoritative research by the Museum

Fig 7. The outlet near Thorney Street on the Embankment near Tate Britain

of London with its deep channels refers to a much earlier period when the post glacier template would have shaped the landscape. After this period streams and channels would have silted up from the Neolithic (4.000 to 2,t00 BCE - Before Common Era-), onwards producing remnant streams which the monks may have eventually cut through. Either way, water from the Tyburn would have reached Thorney Island thanks to either man or Nature. Or both.

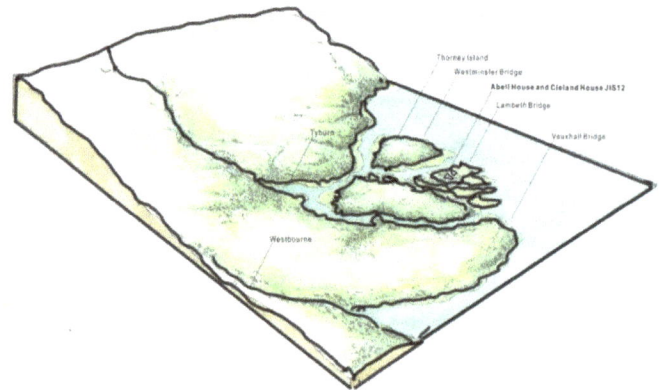

What the convergence of the Tyburn and the Thames might have looked like according to Museum of London archaeologists' research (enhanced from MOLA original)

# 3: The Gatehouse to Heaven - or to Hell

*The ruined Gatehouse in 1776 looking from outside the Abbey towards Tothill Street*

Anyone who walked through this gatehouse, built in 1327, from the end of Tothill Street (seen through the archway) into the main entrance to Westminster Abbey and the heart of Thorney Island, would have got quite a shock. For a start it was not just a gateway to the House of God, it was a prison as well. In fact, there were two prisons, separate but joined together straddling the road. One for the clergy run by the church and the other for run-of-the-mill criminals. You would also have come across a third prison pretty soon after, in the churchyard of St Margaret's. There was a watch house to guard the church, where felons could be kept overnight before being interrogated in the morning.

All this must have seemed to some visitors as a gateway to Hell, not Heaven. In a sense it was true, because at the eastern side of the Precinct running along the wall of Westminster Hall were two taverns called Heaven and Hell, and a third called Purgatory and a fourth, called Paradise. Most of these taverns had been used in their time as prisons, mainly for debtors. That is at least six prisons in all. The Norden map of 1593 (Fig 8) doesn't show the taverns but was the Westminster Shakespeare would have known.

The road immediately outside the Gatehouse was a curved one hugging the outside of the perimeter wall which protected the Abbey and the monastery from the outside world. It was called Thieving Lane (E) not because it was full of thieves, but because it was the route taken to escort new inmates to the Gatehouse prison so they couldn't escape and claim "Sanctuary" in the Abbey precinct.

Sanctuary was an historic practice going back to Saxon times, strongly endorsed by King Edward the Confessor in the eleventh century. It meant that felons of all kinds could claim sanctuary and be protected from arrest.

As a result, the precinct became home to dozens of criminals claiming sanctuary in addition to all the tradespeople and other local inhabitants who lived there. It was completely different from the idealised

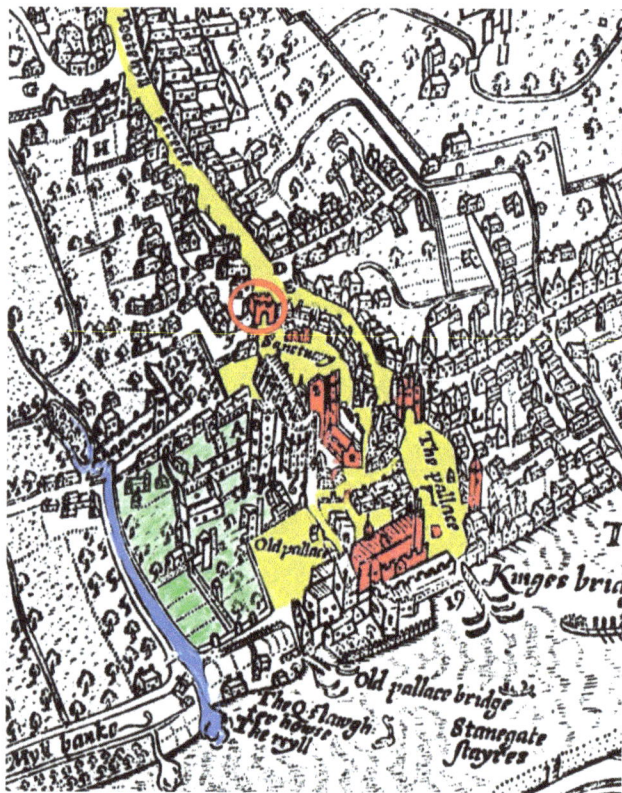

Fig 8. Beneath the Gatehouse (circled in red) is the Bell Tower (much bigger than the etching suggests). In mid photo a second Gatehouse is opposite St Margaret's church leading to King Street (today's Whitehall) and below in "The Palace" (New Palace Yard) is Westminster Hall opposite the Clock Tower (forerunner of Big Ben) with a gallows in between. E is Thieving Lane where felons were taken to the Gatehouse prison. The likely route of the end of Tyburn is in blue. (Norden map of 1593).

Massed dwellings by St Margaret's (in yellow) by Anthony van den Wyngarde in 1542

view of Thorney Island often portrayed in engravings.

In its latter years, the Gatehouse building was just a debtors' prison. We learn from Mr. Mackenzie Walcott's Memorials of Westminster that the debtors "used to let down an alms-box, extended on a pole forty feet long, in order to collect the benevolences of passers-by. They were allowed to buy spirits; and the keeper used to shout from his window to the barman of the neighbouring tavern The Angel, saying: "Jack-ass, jack-ass" thereby signifying the thirst of the prisoners.

The proceedings at the Old Bailey - available online - have lots of references to inmates of the Gatehouse. They include William Cook, a local resident of St Margaret's parish who was executed for counterfeiting the coinage, and John Broccas, believe it or not, the Keeper of The Gatehouse itself, who was accused of High Treason and committed to the King's Bench prison in Southwark. This was because he permitted a Captain William Legg who was imprisoned by Parliament for high treason ("levying war against the King") to escape in October 1642 to rejoin Charles I's army in Oxford.

The Gatehouse was eventually demolished in 1776, following complaints by Dr Johnson and others. He said that "it was so offensive that, without any particular reason, it ought to be pulled down, for it disgraces the present magnificence of the capital, and is a continual nuisance to its neighbours and passengers".

A fascinating thing about the Gatehouse is that, despite being a horrendous prison for hundreds of years, it is mainly remembered today because of two poems written there. One was by Richard Lovelace, a Cavalier poet, and the other by Sir Walter Raleigh the great Elizabethan courtier, historian and buccaneer. Lovelace, who was in prison for trying to get rid of

WEST FRONT OF WESTMINSTER ABBEY, FROM TOTHILL STREET.

*View of the Abbey from Tothill Street*

the Clergy Act of 1640 (which banned bishops and others from having any power in Parliament), wrote a poem to his lover, Althea, including these memorable lines:

Stone walls do not a prison make

Nor iron bars a cage;

Mindes innocent and quiet take

That for an hermitage;

If I have freedome in my love,

And in my soule am free,

Angels alone that sore above

Enjoy such liberty.

It was here too, that Sir Walter Raleigh, suspected of trying to overthrow James I, penned his last poem, or maybe finished an earlier one, on the final night of his life before his execution around the corner in Old Palace Yard on October 29, 1618. It ended:

E'en such is Time! that takes on trust

Our youth, our joys, our all we have,

And pays us but with age and dust;

Who in the dark and silent grave,

When we have wandered all our ways,

Shuts up the story of our days.!

And from which grave, and earth and dust,

The Lord shall raise me up, I trust.

In the morning, Raleigh was taken to Old Palace Yard where he was executed as a traitor and then, bizarrely, treated as a hero by being buried back around the corner under the main altar in St Margaret's church.

Among other later alumni of the Gatehouse was Samuel Pepys, who spent three weeks there in 1690 on suspicion of "being affected" to the exiled royalist King James II.

It seems bizarre to us today that the Abbey could have been associated with such a decrepit prison at the edge of the Sanctuary, but the monks were insulated from the strife. They enjoyed quite a good life inside the monastery with supplies of fresh(ish) food and, judging by archaeological discoveries, a good diet of fish and occasional meat. The Gate House Prison was held on a lease by an individual from the Dean and Chapter. The keeper could keep any fees he charged. He was responsible for the safekeeping of his prisoners, and also for the behaviour of the warders. It was in effect privatised. By the middle of the 18th century, the building was in serious decay and in 1776 an order was made by the Dean and Chapter, for its demolition.

Its remaining inmates were removed from the Gatehouse to the Bridewell House of Correction, which was originally built in 1618 at the other end of today's Victoria Street (by the site of today's Greencoat Boy pub in Greencoat Place). The Gatehouse had survived for 406 years. The Bridewell lasted until 1834 when a new, much larger prison was built on the site where Westminster Cathedral is today.

It is a curious fact that a small part of the 17th century Bridewell prison - to which prisoners of the Gatehouse were moved after its closure - has found its way back to Thorney Island. If you look at the back wall of the Supreme Court there is a stone entrance that goes nowhere. It was one of the entrances to the Bridewell and was rescued by the Greater London Council in 1969 and placed at the back of what was then the Assizes before it became the Supreme Court. It could be viewed as a kind of installation art - a reminder of how this small part of London changed from a place where felons came to escape the law, to where ultimate justice is meted out from which there is no escape. Unless, of course, it becomes a sanctuary again.

*The entrance to the Bridewell House of Correction now at the rear of the Supreme Court*

# 4: The magic of medieval Westminster

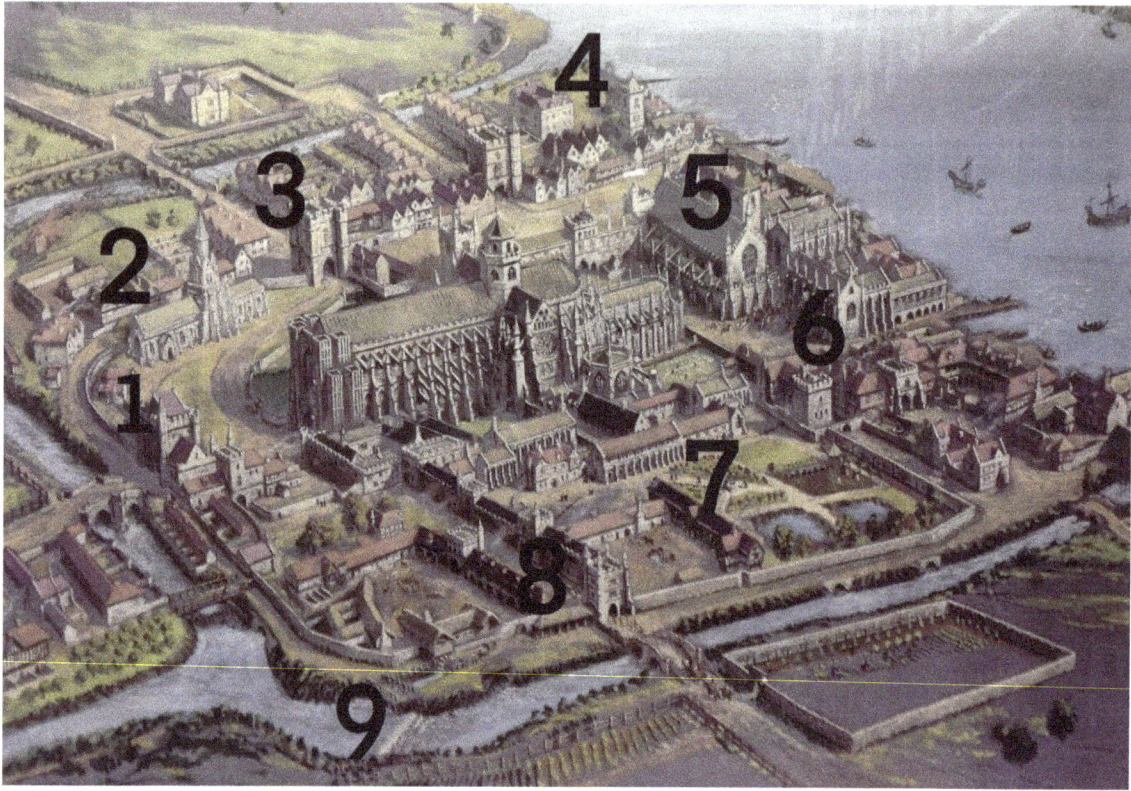

*Artist's view of medieval Thorney Island. The Tothill Street Gatehouse (1), Bell Tower (2), North gate (3), Great Tom (father of Big Ben (4), Westminster Hall (5), Jewel Tower (6), Monastery Garden (7), Southern gatehouse (8), and theTyburn (9). Westminster School is south of the Abbey. Courtesy of Woodmansterne.*

Britain has been gifted by history to be an island surrounded by smaller islands; well over 5,000 of them. The least well known, yet the most important, is right in the heart of London at Westminster. It is called Thorney Island (or Thornea or Torneia or Thornige). The name is a bit of a misnomer as the "ey" at the end of Thorney is short for "eyot" which means a small island so strictly speaking it should really just be called Thorney. It occupies much of the area covered by today's Parliament Square and more. It was called "Thorn" - or Porn (pronounced thorn) in Anglo Saxon times - because of all the brambles that grew there.

It has never been a legal entity, let alone a postcode, and the name was used to describe a wider area than the core island itself. It was arguably formed by the convergence of the River Tyburn with the Thames though you can't see it anymore as the Tyburn is now a subterranean sewer.

On these few acres in central London, much of Britain's history can be traced building by building. Whereas most of the rest of Westminster has been in a state of flux with buildings constantly being pulled down and rebuilt, Thorney, thanks mainly to its status as a World Heritage site, is an island of architectural calm, and it is where the buildings of Westminster Abbey and the Houses of Parliament are located.

For 500 years from King Cnut's first palace, until around 1518, it was the main royal residence until a fire prompted Henry VIII to move and expand his palatial residence into what we know today as Whitehall. It was on Thorney (Island) that Parliament emerged from being a plaything of the monarch to a role model for the English speaking world, and where a modest monastery became Westminster Abbey where every monarch since William the Conqueror has been crowned (and one, Edward V, actually born there). It was here where Westminster School changed from a charity to a fee paying school producing alumni that included Christopher Wren, Isaac Newton and Ben Jonson. Less celebrated is that for nearly 700 years virtually all of our law courts were housed in Westminster Hall and our system of law was exported to most of our colonies including the United States.

Today Thorney Island is almost completely unknown to the general public who pass over it daily in their thousands, because the Tyburn, like all the rivers that once graced the heart of London, has been buried beneath Sir Joseph Bazalgette's life-saving sewer system; but the waters of the Tyburn still roll quietly on. If, for instance, you walk along Great College Street today close to Parliament Square, you are likely walking above part of the Tyburn, now a sewer, though this is still disputed among archaeologists.

No-one doubts it was an island. The question is whether it was formed just by the tidal Thames or the conjunction of the Thames and Tyburn. It once powered the monks' water mill, hence the name Millbank, before emptying its waters into the Thames. Today, those waters are diverted to East End treatment works. (Thank you, Sir Joseph).

Thorney Island isn't an officially designated area. Archaeologists and historians are still arguing about its dimensions but its boundary appears to have expanded from its central core around the Abbey as far as Horseferry Road where the Sanctuary of the Abbey ended. The picture at the top of this chapter is a romanticised vision of what it looked like in medieval times. The river probably looked more like a delta with waters spilling out all over the place, forming lots of smaller islands or eyots.

*The first depiction of Westminster Abbey is on the Bayeux Tapestry c1070*

The origin of Thorney Island can be traced back nearly 3,000 years when global sea levels started to subside. They had previously risen 15 metres as a result of a mega-event when the glaciers melted. That phenomenon had raised sea levels across the planet. Lower levels eventually enabled the Thames, flowing gently from a spring in Oxfordshire, to converge with the Tyburn meandering down from the Hampstead Hills as it still does today, albeit unseen. That, at least, is one version.

Lower sea levels revealed small islands or eyots along the Thames, of which, Thorney was probably the largest. It was composed of compacted sand and gravel sitting on a bed of London clay.

The Tyburn still exists today though its actual course is an ongoing subject for academic debate as a later chapter explains. Much of the original river gets diverted by interceptor channels along the route from the Hampstead hills which redirect its flow to the east end of London to treatment works.

However, in stormy weather the interceptors can't cope and the Tyburn overflows to reach the Thames again through emergency exits. It is still an open question how much of the source waters of the Tyburn actually reach Thorney these days, after so much has been ferried away to treatment works. One way to solve this would be to put an enormous amount of dye at the source in the Hampstead hills and wait to see where it comes out. If only . . .

How long has it been known as Thorney Island? The Museum of London Archaeological Society's Monograph 22 (written after it had done extensive archeological work prior to the construction of the Jubilee Line) states that "it became known in the 8th century as Thorney Island".

This is probably based on a charter of Westminster Abbey attributed to King Offa in 785 AD which referred to a monastery at Torneia (Thorney) "in the terrible place (in loco terriblis) called Westminster". However, this is now accepted by the Abbey as a forgery made

*Westminster Abbey by Wenceslaus Hollar (1607-1677)*

later around 1150 at a time when forgery was a bit of a hobby among the monks wanting to prove ownership of land they thought should be theirs, but to which there was no accessible title. If nothing else, this suggests that the word Torneia, or something similar, was in circulation in 1150 and maybe much earlier.

One of the earliest references in print to Thorney Island was in William of Malmesbury's Gesta Regum Anglorum ("Deeds of the Kings of the English"), circulated in the early 12th century. The Latin text has been translated as "in the marshy place, which is called Thornige (Latin for Thorney), King Edward chose this island to lay the foundation of an abbot and minster there…"

What is certain, according to Westminster Abbey records, is that in about 785 there was a small community of monks on the island, whatever it was called, and that the monastery was enlarged and remodeled after 960 by Saint Dunstan who had become Bishop of London the previous year. St Dunstan founded the monastery, probably on the remains of an earlier church with the help of a vast estate of up to 2,500 acres on the north side of the Thames between the Tyburn and the Fleet which was given to the monks by King Edgar. It effectively covered much of the city of Westminster. It became a Benedictine abbey in the 990s.

In 1016, King Cnut is believed to have been the first monarch to build a palace at Westminster, but the original Abbey owes its origin to (St) Edward the Confessor who built both a palace and a much larger Abbey later in the 11th century. He didn't live to enjoy it as he died in December 1065, and had been too ill to attend the consecration a few days earlier. Henry III later rebuilt it into what it looks like now. Only a few of the foundations of the Confessor's Abbey have survived until today.

Westminster Abbey, or to give it its proper name, The Collegiate College of St Peter, is a mesmeric church, but also a flourishing business thanks to booming tourism which accounts for well over 90% of its income.

The Abbey has not only crowned all monarchs since 1066, it also memorialises hundreds of scientists, aristocrats, authors, actors and other dignitaries within its walls.

It may seem odd that the House of God charges to get in (£30 at the time of writing) while Mammon, in the shape of the nearby Tate Britain, has free entry. The harsh reality is that the Abbey needs all the money it can get to meet the enormous cost of maintaining its structure. As a "royal peculiar" owing allegiance to the Crown rather than the Government, it gets no public money while Tate Britain nearby, thankfully, enjoys a government subsidy.

Most of the medieval buildings are long gone and the remains of others are hidden from public view but one - the Jewel Tower - can still be seen. You don't have to believe that the Island was founded by the mystical appearance of St Peter, as earlier stories claimed, to accept that there is something rather magical about it. If there is any place in Britain or even Europe with such a wealth of history in such a small space, it has yet to reveal itself.

# 5: The Criminal History of the Supreme Court

This drawing is all we have left of Westminster's mighty 60 feet high and 75 feet square Belfry whose bells rang for over 300 years until about 1750. It was situated where the Supreme Court is today in Parliament Square. Built by Edward III (1312-1377), for a time it contained the bells of Westminster Abbey until they were moved to the western towers of the Abbey by Christopher Wren or his assistant Nicholas Hawksmoor. If you were entering the Abbey precinct through the Gate House at the end of Tothill Street, the Belfry would have been the dominant building about 50 yards on your left.

When in full swing its three great bells were so loud that, according to the historian John Stow, they "sowred all the drinke in the towne."

Fig 9

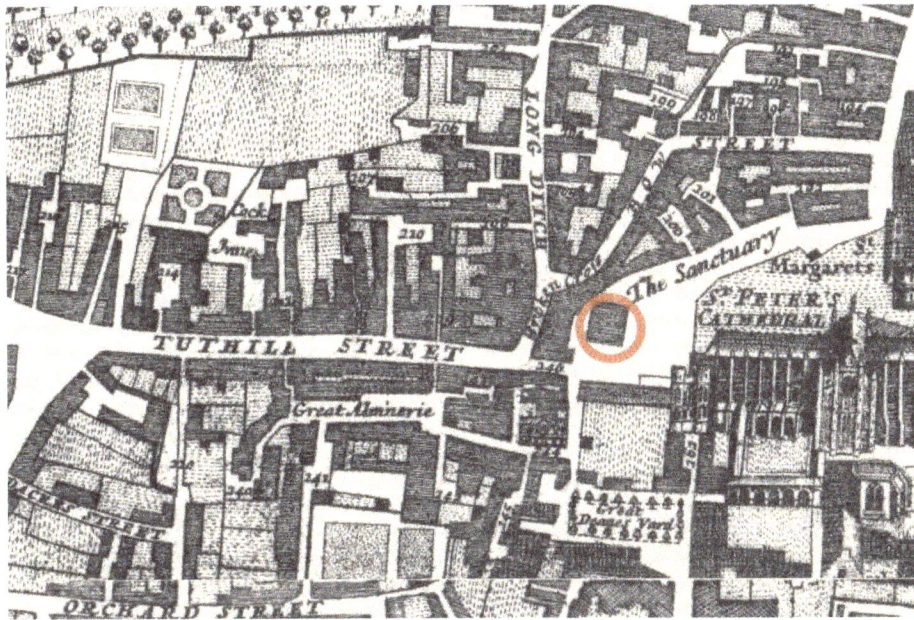

*Morgan's 1592 map. The Bell Tower in red. Tuthill (Tothill) street is there today*

The Supreme Court is the ultimate Court of Appeal to ensure that justice is done. Yet for 400 years the opposite was the case. The Belfry or Bell Tower on this site was regarded as the heart of the "Sanctuary" of Westminster Abbey, a place where felons could escape the arm of the law as long as they confessed their wrongdoing. Not even the monarch could ignore this right of sanctuary which was firmly established by King (or St) Edward the Confessor in the 11th century, though the origin was much earlier in Saxon times. The area of sanctuary, technically, extended way beyond the walled precincts of the Abbey. It included much of today's Parliament Square and extended right down to Strutton Ground and Horseferry Road, though it must have been very difficult to police it at that distance. Although the core of Thorney Island was the centre of Old Westminster, the wider definition probably followed the contours of the Sanctuary.

Tim Tatton Brown in his contribution to the book Westminster – the Art, Architecture and Archaeology of the Royal Abbey and Palace, suggests that this wider area may have marked the late Anglo-Saxon boundary of the Monastery's land. He adds: "It is even possible that this larger area, with the Royal Vill (an administrative center shared between the royal court and local people) and its vast new Abbey church in the north east corner, was the original "Thorney Island".

Most abbeys had sanctuaries. The one on Thorney Island was bigger than most and lasted until James I finally abolished it. However, the culture of criminality that it created lasted for centuries afterwards. It didn't disappear, it just moved nearby which was why the area behind today's Victoria Street was so ridden with crime and prostitution that it became known as "The Devil's Acre", a phrase popularised by Charles Dickens. (See Chapter 27 Devils Acre).

There are hardly any reproductions of the Bell Tower, except for a sketch (Fig 9) made by William Stukely, an eminent archeologist who rushed to record it when the building was being demolished. He wrote: "On November 14, 1750, I went to survey the old church at Westminster called The Sanctuary which they were then pulling down to make a new market house. The building itself is as extraordinary in its kind, as that we have no clear account concerning it in the history of Westminster Abbey to which it manifestly belongs."

It had only one door and one window on the ground floor, but two chapels on different floors where refugees could hear mass and hopefully put themselves on the road to redemption. Its history is preserved in today's street names such as The Sanctuary and Little Sanctuary, which meander around the side of the Supreme Court.

*Fig 10. The bell tower at Salisbury Cathedral is similar to the one that was on Thorney Island. (Wenceslaus Hollar (1607-1677)*

The Supreme Court stands on the remains of two previous Guildhall buildings dating to the early and late 19th centuries. Foundations of the medieval structure and earlier Saxon remains were uncovered by archaeologists in 1912. Some believe that more remains might be waiting to be discovered. This seems unlikely in view of the depth of the building, but there may be some nearby. It is not a well known fact, but the Court has a pleasant café in the basement which is open to the public as is the Court itself when it is in session.

What the engraving does not show is that above it there would have been three other layers including a bell tower and a spire. It was apparently similar to a tower at Salisbury Cathedral of which there is an engraving (Fig 10). This was executed by the great Czech artist Wenceslaus Hollar, who, as it happens, was a resident of Thorney Island in Gardener Street. He died there in 1677 in such poverty that he had to beg the bailiffs not to take his bed before he died. He was buried in the churchyard of St Margaret's Church.

The Bell Tower was built as a fortress with thick walls to resist possible attack. There were also bells in the cloisters of nearby St Stephen's Chapel dating from even earlier times and also at St Margaret's Church adjacent to the Abbey, not to mention the Clock Tower in New Palace Yard which housed the predecessor of Big Ben. Bells, bells everywhere.

The belfry, or a part of it, was afterwards converted into a tavern called The Three Tuns with its vaults serving as a wine-cellar. It was also called The Castle at some stage. The building was demolished around 1750, and on part of its site a meat-market was built. The market was later removed and in its place the Middlesex Guildhall, or Sessions House was constructed.

Today, its successor, the Supreme Court, stands confidently on the site of the Belfry from where it administers final judgment. But it can't escape its history. It stands on the remains of the lawless Bell Tower where criminals could escape justice. What it must have been like to live in this extraordinary fusion of religion and wildlife can only be imagined. However, ordinary life somehow went on.

And where there is ordinary life, it would have been no surprise to find Samuel Pepys whose diary recorded a number of visits to Westminster, not least when he married his wife Elizabeth in a civil ceremony on December 1, 1655 in St Margaret's Church.

Pepys lived in nearby Axe Yard for a short period and was a frequent visitor to the area as Secretary of the Admiralty and also as MP for Harwich. He was imprisoned for a time in the Gatehouse Prison under suspicion of Jacobinism and on 3rd August 1660 he recalled that he had dined in a curiously named tavern known as the Quaker's Tavern in the Great Sanctuary because it had been leased by the Dean and Chapter to a man known as a Quaker who sold wine in draught. It may well have been the Three Tuns under a nickname.

At the back of the Supreme Court building in Little Sanctuary today you will find the stone doorway to the Tothill Fields Bridewell prison which used to be at the other end of Victoria Street next to today's Greencoat pub (where Artillery Row meets Greycoat Place). The doorway was moved to this site by the Greater London Council in 1969. What happened to the rest of the prison is not known. The doorway could be regarded as a piece of installation art, an unintended reminder to the Supreme Court of its criminal history. Felons who pass through a gateway to a prison might well find their case ends up in the Supreme Court.

If the sanctuary existed today, you could be sure that

*The gateway to Tothill Street prison in Little Sanctuary*

immigrants in fear of being deported would make a beeline for it and, if the laws of the day were observed, not even the courts could have done anything about it. One can't escape the irony of the Supreme court, the pinnacle of English justice, being on the site of a sanctuary where you could have escaped justice with the entrance to a prison now tacked on to it.

# 6: How Green's Alley started a beer revolution

Green's Alley, situated in the medieval precinct of Westminster Abbey, must be one of the least known lanes in London's history, yet it marked the birth of what eventually became one of the biggest drinks companies on the planet. It is usually mentioned on maps by a number and only rarely, as in the Rocque map of 1746 (Fig 11), is it given the courtesy of an actual name. In this patch of the Broad Sanctuary, the Greens (or Greenes), after whom the alley was presumably named, had a brewhouse with associated inns in the Sanctuary and in nearby King Street (today's Whitehall) as far back as the early 1400s.

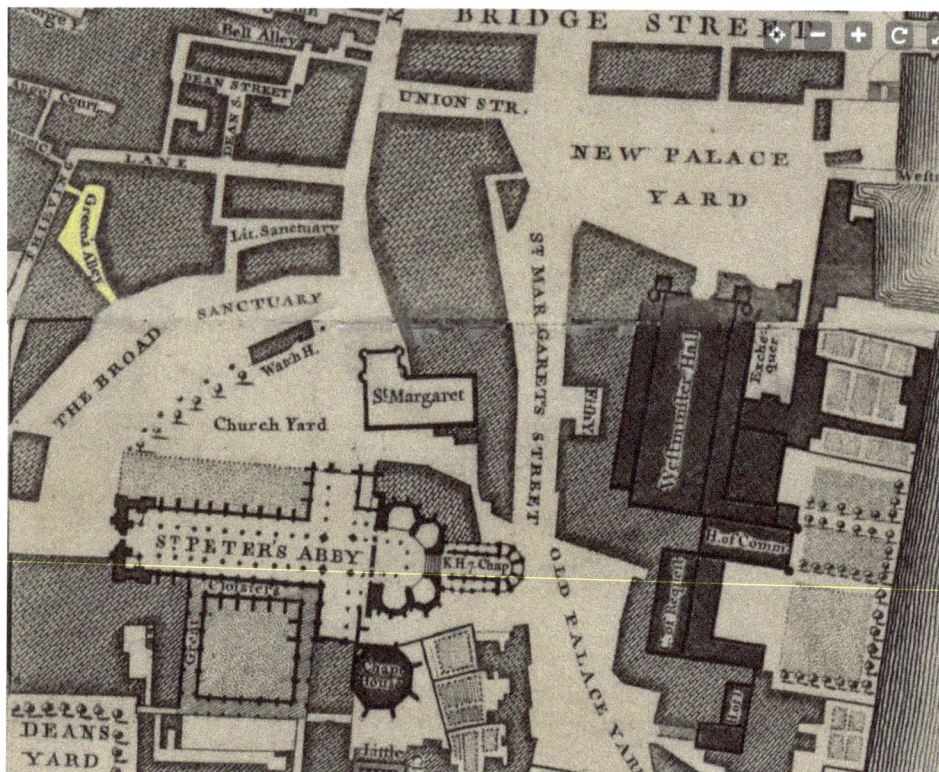
Fig 11. Rocque's map 1746 with Green's Alley in yellow

In his book The Red Barrel: A history of Watney Mann, Hurford Janes observed: "In or near the Broad Sanctuary, the Greene family continued to brew beer and to prosper. The records of the Abbey show granting or renewal of countless properties in this area. The long vanished Green's Alley, now dominated by such figures as Abraham Lincoln and Benjamin Disraeli, took its name from the tenure of what was once Abbey land".

Actual dates are rare, but as far back as 1420 Thomas Greene, was elected Master of the Brewers's Company Company, and so may have been brewing years before at Westminster which seems to have been the centre of his early operations. Most of the subsequent Green(e)s seem to have been called John or William. At one stage, John Green held the Nag's Head, the Chequers, the Raven, the Windmill and the Buffalo's Head in King Street while William is reported to have relinquished occupation of the Talbot (later the Three Tuns) next to the medieval Gatehouse in 1607 after occupying it for 40 years.

What makes this unusual is that it is possible to trace the corporate DNA of Diageo, one of the world's largest drinks companies, to the Greens' activities in the medieval Broad Sanctuary. Diageo's huge portfolio of alcoholic drinks includes Guinness and the lion's share of all Scotch whisky companies. Expansion started when the Greenes moved from their roots in Broad Sanctuary to the other end of today's Victoria Street where they established the Stag brewery near where Marks and Spencer is today and where until recently there was a Stag Place. A stag was the motto of the Green family.

The brewery belonged to the Greene family until 1787 and it didn't do badly. In 1722 it was described as being "the finest Brewhouse in Europe". Expansion gathered pace and in 1837 James Watney, a miller from Wandsworth, bought a quarter share and became a partner with another local brewer, John Lettsom Elliott. For a while the premises were known as Elliot Watney and Company (Fig 12). The entrance was at the end of today's Castle Lane, which used to be called Cabbage Lane and had two alleys running

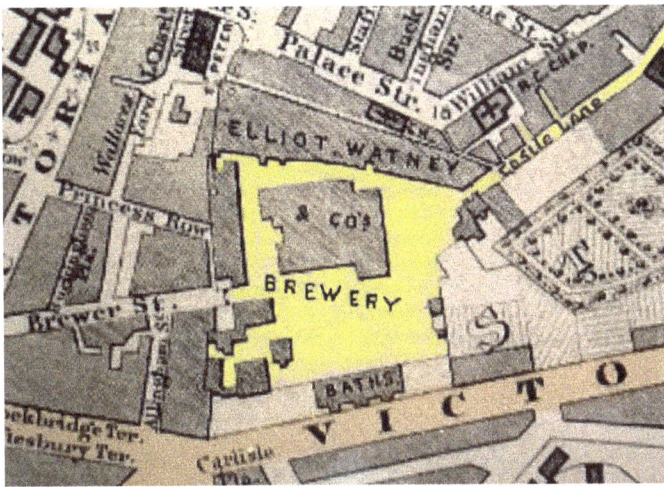

*Fig 12.*

off it, called Powder Beef Court and Mustard Alley. The site was opposite today's Victoria Palace theatre, where a branch of Marks and Spencer currently takes up part of the space.

By 1858 the brewery was under James Watney's control until his death, aged well over 80, in 1884. After his death, Watney & Co started a prolonged period of merger mania. The fusion of Watney with Combe and Co of Long Acre and then Reid's stout of Clerkenwell into Watney, Combe & Reid was reckoned to have been the first big merger in the history of British brewing. In 1958 came an even bigger union when Watney merged with Mann, Crossman & Paulin to form Watney Mann. That wasn't the end of it.

In 1972, Grand Metropolitan, the huge hotel and hospitality group, acquired Watney Mann. Grand Met later merged these acquisitions with Truman Hanbury Buxton. An even bigger merger happened in 1997 when Diageo was formed through the merger of the iconic Guinness plc - which can trace its own ancestry back to 1759 - with Grand Metropolitan plc, creating one of the world's largest producers of alcoholic beverages. The merger combined Guinness's brewing and spirits expertise with Grand Metropolitan's extensive portfolio in food, beverages, and hospitality.

Why is it called Diageo? The word combines the Latin word Dies (day) with the Greek geo (meaning work or earth). The Stag brewery lasted until 1959, well within the memory of some local residents, but was deemed too small for the enlarged company's needs and was closed down. Watney had achieved considerable success with its alliterative slogan "What We Want is Watneys" but ran into trouble when the emerging Campaign for Real Ale went for it and other brewers in a big way, with sustained criticism of its huge promotion of the Red Barrel keg beer.

Nothing remains of the brewery building. An old photo (Fig 13) shows the site of the Stag Tap pub in Castle Lane, which was used by brewery employees, and Westminster Archives has produced photographic records of what it was like to work there including YouTube videos. The buildings to the rear of the pub in the picture, including the Westminster Chapel, are still functioning.

The only structure surviving from the earlier Greene era is the beautiful Wren-like Bluecoat (Blewcoat) school in Brewers Green, Caxton Street, which was built in 1709 by William Greene, partly to educate the children of employees, but also to keep barrels of beer in the basement. The name Brewers' Green is almost certainly a pun on the connections of the Green(e) family to this historic place.

Christopher Wren was associated with the school and may well have been the architect as it was in his style and according to Hurford Janes in his History of Watneys: "The architect had every reason to be grateful to a man who made it possible for his grand design for the Royal Hospital to attain fulfilment". The

Fig 13

The Wren influenced Blewcoat school of 1709

Greens apparently owned some of the land on which Wren's hospital was built.

William Greene was also one of the founders of the Westminster Infirmary which later became the Westminster Hospital. He joined other philanthropists led by Sir Henry Hoare of Hoare's Bank to create a hospital for poorer people who at the time had no access to health care. The work of Sir Henry and his colleagues, explained elsewhere, helped to lay the foundations of a voluntary hospital which marked an important stage in the emergence of public healthcare in Britain.

# 7. A glimpse of medieval New Palace Yard

*Fig 14. Wenceslaus Hollar's engraving of New Palace Yard in 1647*

This part of the North Precinct of the Abbey is known as New Palace Yard because it was new when William II ("Rufus") planned to have a new palace constructed there around 1097. It was called "new" to distinguish it from Old Palace Yard built by King Edward the Confessor fifty years earlier.

In the end the only part of the plan that was actually built (in 1097) was Westminster Hall on the extreme left of the engraving which is still there today in all its glory. To get one's bearings right - in the main engraving (Fig 14) we are looking at Westminster Hall as if we were standing where the entrance to Westminster Tube station is today along Bridge Street. And the white area in the middle? Today that covers a 5-storey underground car park for 450 vehicles for MPs. No kidding.

The images (Fig 14 & 15) were drawn by Wenceslaus Hollar, the great Czech artist and engraver in 1647 probably while he was abroad in Antwerp during the English civil war, which went on between1642 and 1651. Hollar died in extreme poverty on March 25, 1677 in Gardener's Lane close to where he drew this picture. He is buried in St Margaret's Church. It is because of Hollar's priceless etchings that we have these unique engravings of Thorney Island.

It is an illustration to conjure with. This is partly because of what is still there. Westminster Hall remains today in exactly the same place enabling us to know where the other remains were located. It is partly because of what is not there - the Clock Tower on the extreme right of both pictures, the predecessor of Big Ben, which has long since been demolished. It was situated near where Big Ben is today. However, a key part of it - its huge bell (Great Tom) - remains to this day in St Paul's Cathedral. What is also not there is the Grand Conduit or fountain (in front of the Clock Tower in the main

*Fig 15. The Clock Tower and Westminster Hall (in yellow) from across the Thames (Hollar)*

Hollar etching, Fig 14), the remains of which should be there but are not having been moved into storage. In the background to the top right of the fountain is the entrance to New Palace Yard, supposedly built by Richard lll during his short reign in 1483-85 and located where the statue of Winston Churchill is today. Nothing remains of that.

*The gatehouse, Clock Tower, the Conduit and Westminster Hall are in colour (Agas map 1560-1570)*

# 8: Two old Etonians clash over a wine-spouting fountain

Wenceslaus Hollar's depiction of the Grand Conduit in New Palace Yard (Fig 16) was a tragedy from an archaeological point of view. No one seems to have known it was there when the Government decided in the 1970s to tear the place apart to provide space for - wait for it - a five-storey underground park for 450 cars for MPs.

The government of the day was dismissive of any possible archaeological finds.

No digging was allowed, only a reluctant permission for archaeologists to keep "a watching brief". Which they did, and what they found was remarkable in the circumstances: the huge octagonal base of a canopied fountain as seen in purple in front of the clock tower

Fig 16: The Grand Conduit (red) with the Gatehouse, (blue) where Churchill's statue is today in Parliament Square and the Clock Tower (yellow, right) near where Big Ben is today

on Hollar's engraving. It had been built by Henry VI in 1443 and contained marble slabs, the remains of an earlier 12th century conduit. The fountain lasted until the late 17th century. It is not known how high it was but judging from Hollar's impression it was far higher than the local people who look tiny in comparison and looked nearly as tall as nearby houses.

As the only secular fountain in the area not linked to a

church or monastery, it would have been used by local people as part of the everyday life of medieval London and, doubtless, a popular source of local gossip, the equivalent of today's water cooler talk in the office. It supplied water to the royal palace as well as the ordinary folk of Westminster.

Henry VI had granted permission to the parish to make use of the surplus water; in 1524 there is this

*Uncovering the Grand Conduit (MOLA)*

mention in the churchwardens' accounts: "The King's Charter for the Condett at the Pales'gate remayneth in the custody of the Churchwardens." Occasionally, something more dramatic happened. According to the medieval historian, John Stow, on special occasions such as the coronation of Edward II in 1307, it was "made to run with wine out of divers, spouts." Apparently it was "a beautiful fountain, the water of which fell in large cascades."

Sometime between 1658 and 1660, just before the Restoration of the Monarchy, the Great Conduit in New Palace yard was demolished, but, fortunately, its memory - and its location - had been fixed by Hollar a few years earlier.

We should be grateful that remains of the Great Conduit fountain have been preserved in storage but it is so sad, not to say outrageous, that they weren't preserved on the site itself. This didn't happen because politicians were opposed to letting the archaeologists loose. What might they get up to? It is a puzzle why neither the Government nor archaeologists appear to have used the Hollar drawing - which has proved pretty accurate in most respects - as a reason to excavate more carefully in the area where the conduit was likely to be. The Government wanted a huge car park for MPs and that was that.

The matter was discussed in the Commons by - who else?- two old Etonians. On 29th November 1972, Paul Channon, Conservative Minister for Housing and Construction told Tam Dalyell (Labour, West Lothian) that delay would be "expensive and inconvenient" and could only be justified if there were "really important and closely defined archaeological objectives in view". That was probably intended to exclude everything. However, although archaeologists managed to secure a "watching brief" they were unable to preserve this fascinating artefact in its original place. It is now being kept somewhere in storage, a memory of Thorney Island waiting to be restored. There are other parts of Edward the Confessor's palace in Old Palace Yard which are believed to be lying underground in the vicinity of the statue of Richard the Lionheart. Let us hope that when the upcoming restoration of Parliament takes place, politicians will have a greater regard for the preservation of our heritage.

# 9: The history of Britain in one building

*Westminster Hall with shops on both sides*

Richard II, son of the Black Prince, who was King of England from 1377 until 1399, made a lasting impression on Thorney Island. He had a stunning hammerbeam roof put over the structure of the existing Westminster Hall which had been built by William Rufus, son of William the Conqueror. Now, over 600 years later, the hammerbeam roof is still richly admired as one of the biggest and most beautiful roofs of its kind in the world.

Richard himself was not so lucky. He was deposed on 30th September 1399 by the future Henry IV before his improvements had been completed - and his deposition took place inside his own reconstructed hall. Richard died a year later in suspicious circumstances, probably starved to death, but he left permanent marks in the Hall which is festooned with load-supporting corbels carved with his own emblems.

Thorney Island took its own revenge. When Henry IV was nearing the end of his life he decided to undergo a pilgrimage to Jerusalem to atone for his sins, not least his usurpation of the throne of Richard II He believed a prophecy in Holinshed's Chronicles that he would "not die but in Jerusalem". In 1413, on his way to the Holy Land, he stopped off at Westminster Abbey to pray at the tomb of St Edward the Confessor where he collapsed. He was taken to the nearby Jerusalem Chamber where he did indeed die, thereby fulfilling Holinshed's prophecy in an unexpected manner. (Insert cross ref)

Not even Holinshead could have prophesied what Westminster Abbey experienced thereafter. Dorian Gerhold, the historian, sums it up:

"Nowhere else in the world is there a building which has been so closely involved in the life of a nation for such a long period. The history of the hall was therefore almost a history of England and of Great Britain".

But where to start and where to finish? The trial and execution of Charles 1, or that of Sir William "Braveheart" Wallace, or Sir Thomas More, or Guy Fawkes? Oliver Cromwell was not tried there, but after the Restoration of the Monarchy in May, 1660, his body was exhumed and his head affixed to a pole on one of the towers of the hall where it stayed for over 25 years as a warning to anyone thinking of deposing a king. It was then passed through private collections before being buried in 1960 at a secret location at his former college Sidney Sussex in Cambridge.

This left Charles l, who was buried at Windsor Castle, a long way from the man who had him executed. Except that Thorney Island had other ideas. Cromwell has a statue outside Westminster hall. If you look immediately across the road on the eastern wall of St Margaret's Church there is a small lead bust of none

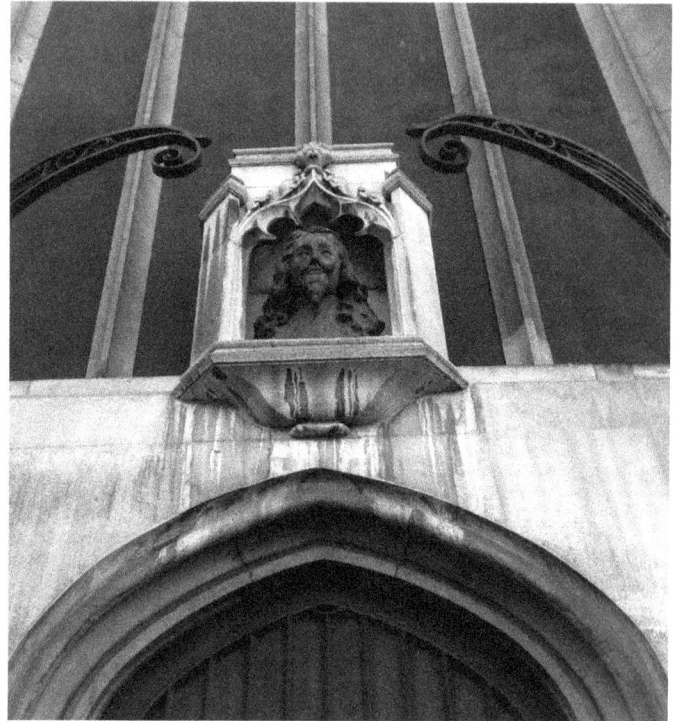

*Charles I looking at Cromwell from the wall of St Margaret's Church*

other than Charles I attached to the wall glaring at his executioner.

Charles I is buried in St George's Chapel at Windsor Castle. After his execution on 30th January 1649, his body was interred there on 9th February 1649, following a decision by Parliament to deny him burial in Westminster Abbey to prevent public unrest. His remains were placed in the same burial vault as Henry VIII and Jane Seymour.

The impeachment of Warren Hastings, the first Governor of Bengal, at Westminster Hall in 1787 for corruption, was described in the King's Works as "one of the most extraordinary legal proceedings on record". It adds: "20 volumes of parliamentary reports, 11 folio volumes of evidence, 3,000 pages of oratory, 20 years of agitation, memorable performances by

Burke, Fox and Sheridan all resulting in an acquittal seven years after the start of the trial". Protector Somerset, Lord Protector of England from 1547 to 1549 during the minority of Edward VI, was not so lucky. He was acquitted of treason but executed for a felony.

These incidents happened during an astonishing period of almost 700 years when Westminster Hall, besides having nearly 50 shops, also housed all the main courts and played a pivotal role in the development of the English legal system. This included the rule of law and trial by jury which in turn influenced legal systems around the world, especially in the colonies including the American Constitution and Bill of Rights.

One person who was not granted trial by jury was Charles I, who in 1649 was tried by a special court in Westminster Hall but not allowed to say a word in his defence. English justice took a brief holiday.

The law courts stayed in Westminster Hall until after the Great Fire of 1834 which devastated the Houses of Parliament but left Westminster Hall intact thanks to favourable winds and special instructions to fire fighters to preserve the historic hall at all costs. However, it was realised soon after that overcrowding had become a serious problem and it was decided to move the Courts of Law and Equity, Divorce, Probate and Bankruptcy into one location in the Strand. Some 700 years of tradition moved on.

Of all the amazing things that happened in Westminster Hall, one tiny thing keeps coming back to me. In 1904 some of the oak beams needed replacing. Offers from Australia and Ireland were turned down as English oak was preferred. Things looked grim until George Courthope whose, Wadhurst family estate - can you believe it - had supplied many of the oak trees 600 years earlier, offered replacements. Later on, during a debate on the Forestry Commission Courthope, now

*Oliver Cromwell outside Westminster Hall*

an MP, revealed that the replacement beams had over 600 annual rings. In other words they were already growing when the original trees were felled. If you know of a better example of longtermism it would be good to know.

33

# 10: The teeming taverns of the Green Yard

*The Green Yard*

If you look at early engravings of Thorney Island, they reflect a solemn silence and an eerie absence of social activity, which is unsurprising in the precincts of an Abbey. However, nothing could be further from the truth. Whereas today's Parliament Square has no pubs at all (St Stephen's Tavern at the northern end is outside the Square) medieval Westminster was teeming with them, as politicians, clerics, lawyers, Palace employees, criminals, and other hucksters indulged themselves at any opportunity.

The so-called Green Yard, linking Old Palace Yard with New Palace Yard, is a comparatively small area running along St Margaret's Lane and Abingdon Street hugging the side of Westminster Hall (above), yet it had an astonishing ten pubs. It is not clear how many were there at the same time, but it seems most of them would have been.

One of the more recent was the Star and Garter, at 4 Old Palace Yard on the Abbey side of the yard where recorded records go back to 1787. More recently William Wilberforce, the abolitionist, lived at number 4.

The most notorious of the taverns, mainly on the other side of the street straddling Westminster Hall were the bizarrely named Heaven, Hell, Purgatory, and Paradise. It must have sounded like the scenes from a medieval miracle play. All of these competed in the constrained space of Old Palace Yard for custom, along with The Coach and Horses, the Royal Oak and the White Rose, not to mention coffee houses such as Waghorne's, Oliver's, and Alice's, (a popular place for lawyers and politicians which lasted until the great fire of 1834).

The most notorious tavern was Hell, appropriately situated in a subterranean passage near Purgatory close by Westminster Hall abutting the Exchequer. Heaven and Hell were both popular from the 16th to the 18th centuries and both had been debtors' prisons. Hell had once been a torture chamber where the King tried to force inmates to pay off their debts before being released. It was the haunt of many shady characters, including lowly lawyers' clerks like Dapper in Ben Jonson's celebrated play The Alchemist who was forbidden "to break his fast in Heaven or Hell".

Samuel Pepys dismissed the tavern Hell as a "resort of disreputable characters and the most raffish of lawyers' clerks", though the food was supposed to have been surprisingly good.

A contemporary poem (unknown author) gives a local flavour:

"Hence we to HELL in Westminster advance,

Where LAWYERS, not the DEVIL lead the dance;

Where Litigant, outrageous for their Fees,

Unmercifully, Clients Pockets squeeze (etc)".

Hell's most notorious contribution to history was on December 6, 1648, when a band of soldiers prevented members of Parliament from entering the House of Commons during the Civil War (1642 to 1651). The previous day, Parliament had voted by

129 to 83 to continue negotiating with King Charles I in the hope of reaching a compromise. Even though Charles had been defeated in the first period of civil war, he still retained bargaining power not least among moderate Parliamentarians. This was not what Oliver Cromwell wanted and a detachment under Colonel Thomas Pride refused entry to 180 MPs including all 129 who wanted to continue negotiating with the King. This move became known as Pride's Purge and it paved the way to get a parliamentary majority to execute the King. In the end, the vote to stop negotiating with Charles was taken by only 83 MPs, an extraordinary assault on democracy. Many of the MPs were imprisoned overnight in Hell and in other houses along the Strand. One can only imagine how the course of history would have changed if the vote had been conducted in a democratic manner.

Heaven, though close to Hell at the north end of Lindsay Lane (now called Abingdon Street), appears to have been a slightly more upmarket operation. It was good enough for Pepys who went there with a friend on January 28,1660 and noted in his diary: "And so I returned and went to Heaven, where Ludlin and I dined."

Purgatory must also have been a rough prison in its time. According to John Timbs in his Club Life of London, Purgatory kept "ducking stools for scolds (prostitutes), who were placed in a chair fastened on an iron pivot to the end of a long pole, which was balanced at the middle upon a high trestle, thus allowing the culprit's body to be ducked in the Thames".

Not much is known about the people who actually lived in Old Palace Yard apart from William Wilberforce, who lived at 4 Old Palace Yard from 1786 to 1808 (to the left of today's statue of George V).

An interesting exception was James Edward Oglethorpe, a Tory politician who lived close to

*Oglethorpe's tree-fronted home in Old Palace Yard*

Heaven and Hell. He is mainly remembered for founding the colony of Georgia in North America. In 1731, he was made a director of the Royal African Company, England's biggest slave trading operation, but he appears to have had a change of heart when he purchased the freedom of an enslaved African trader called Ayuba Suleiman Diallo after seeing a letter written by him. Oglethorpe seems to have lost interest in Diallo after that, but the experience led him to resign from the Royal African Company and after arriving in Georgia he instituted a ban on slavery.

He also banned alcohol (which would not have been popular in Old Palace Yard). He hoped to settle what were called England's "worthy poor" in Georgia starting with those in prison for debts.

Oglethorpe's action in banning slavery when Georgia was founded in 1733 was well before more celebrated abolitionists such as Wilberforce. However, the prohibition seems to have been largely ignored after Oglethorpe left Georgia in 1743. A huge opportunity for Britain to have taken an earlier lead in abolishing slavery was lost.

# 11: The History of Parliament in half a dozen buildings

England may or may not be the Mother of Parliaments - a phrase conjured up by John Bright in the 18th century - but she was at the very least a vital incubator, a story that can be told through half a dozen buildings on Thorney Island, most of which can still be seen today intact or as ruins.

When was the first parliament? UNESCO says the first modern parliament in Europe, with the presence of the common people through elected representatives, was in 1188 when Alfonso IX, King of Leon (in Spain) convened the three states in the Cortes of León.

The Althing in Iceland, was established even earlier in 930 AD. It has a good claim to be the oldest surviving parliament, but it lost its power in 1262 after Iceland's union with Norway. It wasn't revived until Iceland gained home rule from Denmark in 1904 leaving a gap of over 600 years when it didn't exist.

England wasn't far behind. The Westminster model goes back a long way and has influenced the governance of many nations, mainly those that were once part of the British Empire, including Australia, the United States, New Zealand, Canada, India, Malaysia, and Jamaica, all of which have adopted variations of the Westminster system.

At the heart of the problem is the question - What do we mean by "Parliament"? If we just mean the King being stripped of much of his power, then an influential event was in 1253 when Henry III swore on the Gospel to keep to the Magna Carta, signed by King John at Runnymede in 1215, but which had been ill-observed since then.

This happened within Westminster Abbey in St Catherine's Chapel, the considerable remains of which can be seen at the end of the Little Cloister. But this was not a real parliament anymore than Runnymede was as the general population was not represented.

So where did it all start in the UK? J R Maddicott in his much praised The Origins of the English Parliament, 924 to 1327 sees the Anglo-Saxon

*Remains of the wall of the refectorywhere Paliament cut its teeth seen from upstairs in the Abbey's Cellarium café*

*The remains of St Catherine's Chapel where Henry III endorsed the Magna Carta*

A key stage in the growth of a modern Parliament is often thought to be 1258 in Oxford when nobles led by Simon De Montfort (who had been born and bred in France) drafted the Provisions of Oxford This stripped Henry III of his unrestrained authority and placed him under the guidance of 24 people (all men) of whom half were nominated by the King and half by the "reformers", mainly De Montfort's supporters. The document called for regular Parliaments with representatives from the counties. This was an important development in the evolution of Parliament, but as it mainly consisted of nobles, De Montfort's allies, and gentry, it is not regarded as a lasting precursor of today's populist Parliament.

In 1264, De Montfort roundly defeated his former friend, King Henry III, at the Battle of Lewes and afterwards seized power. For a year he was the unelected ruler of Britain, having gained power by imprisoning his own King. He summoned a parliament on January 20, 1265, most likely in the Chapter House. For the first time not only were churchmen, barons, and two knights from each shire summoned, but also two commoners from each of the boroughs. Technically, this was a milestone as it was the first known assembly in this country at which both the town and the country were represented at the same meeting, but it was not democratic. It was packed with de Montfort's cronies to boost his power against rival nobles and the King was his prisoner.

He was using Parliament not for the general good, but to bolster his own grip on government by including cronies and other loyalists to defeat the increasing number of barons opposed to him. He also expelled and massacred the Jews, hardly a role model of someone concerned with building a modern parliament.

In 1295, the so-called Model Parliament was called in the Palace of Westminster, which probably meant Westminster Hall. Edward I, "Longshanks", desperately

Witan as the earliest origin of England's modern Parliament, as it "began the process of allowing small collections of representatives to set the laws for the whole country". They were held around the country and when in London they used Westminster Hall.

This didn't really count as a Parliament in the modern sense as it was peripatetic and there were no widely elected representatives of ordinary people there. It wasn't primarily about raising taxes except on special occasions like the imposition of Danegeld on the nobles (protection money to prevent Viking invasions).

needed money for his wars in Scotland and France. It has been regarded as a model for the future because it contained not only the higher ranks of clergy and gentry, but also the "lower orders" of clergy plus two citizens from each city and two burgesses from each borough. However, most of these constituents were not exactly representative of the people at large and can be traced to earlier parliaments.

More importantly, the "Commons" on this occasion met separately from the upper ranks which proved a template for the emergence of a true democracy. It wasn't truly representative of the people as there was no widespread suffrage and its "model" excluded half of the population: Women.

In April 1343, another staging post was reached. It was the first time when the meeting place of the lower house or Commons was actually recorded. It was when Edward III opened parliament in the wonderfully ornate Painted Chamber with its warlike scenes from the bible (tapestry above) after which he and the top brass withdrew, leaving the Commons alone until they had finished their business. It has been estimated that 41 meetings of Parliament were held there between 1399 and 1484.

*The Painted Chamber*

The Good Parliament of 1376, also held in the Painted Chamber, is linked to the Peasants' Revolt of 1381, through its exposure of governmental corruption and the subsequent failure to implement lasting reforms. The parliament's efforts to address corruption were reversed by John of Gaunt, leading to public dissatisfaction. This disillusionment, combined with economic hardships and oppressive imposts such as the Poll Tax, fueled the grievances that erupted in the Peasants' Revolt, during which John of Gaunt's London home, the Savoy Palace, was looted and burned. It is remembered today by the Savoy Hotel which is on part of the same site.

Sadly, the Painted Chamber has long been demolished though, according to historian David Harrison, the remains could still survive under Old Palace Yard east of the statue of Richard the Lionheart. He also believes that the remains of the Lesser Hall or White Hall, used for meetings of the House of Lords, could be under the north side of the same statue awaiting discovery by archaeologists.

After the Painted Chamber, the Commons was shunted between the Chapter House, where the monks met each day to conduct their business, spiritual or temporal, and the monks' refectory where they had their meals. MPs had to make sure they had finished their politics before the monks needed it for their meals. The Refectory became the regular meeting-place of the Commons until the Dissolution of the Monasteries when they moved across the road into the newly secularised St Stephen's Chapel in 1548.

It was in the Chapter House and the Refectory that the Commons cut its teeth - and both buildings, in part or in whole, can be viewed today. The Chapter House was where the monks met daily to read a "chapter" from the rules of St Benedict before discussing the religious business of the day. It wasn't very convenient for the monks who couldn't use it while MPs were in

*The Chapter House*

In 1540, after the Reformation had terminated its religious use, St Stephen's Chapel, courtesy of the Protestant Edward IV, became the first permanent home of the Commons. The new building retained the earlier layout with lines of monks facing each other on benches, a fact that is often blamed for the confrontational way the main parties do business with each other today.

However, judging by contemporary accounts, the behaviour of the Commons while sitting was far worse even than it is today, not helped by the fact that bills and other legislation were read out in full to all the members who could stay awake. Readings were necessary in the early days because many MPs were illiterate.

David Harrison, a historian of Westminster, says that MPs were much criticised being seen as "useless and impotent". Some were accused of vandalism. The refectory was demolished in 1544, but the remains of one long wall are preserved in the garden of

session and it definitely wasn't convenient for MPs as there could be 200 or even 300 of them in a confined space normally used by a maximum of 80 monks. In those days, meetings of MPs must have seemed a bit like Damon Runyon's floating crap game in Guys and Dolls. They had to find rooms that happened to be available.

The monks' refectory at Westminster Abbey had been used by Parliament for short periods in the late 13th century, but in 1397 the House of Commons moved there and used it as its regular base after vacating the Chapter House. This marked the permanent return of the Chapter House to the monks.

The monks were pleased to have their Chapter House back, but the much bigger refectory did not lead to harmonious relations. Apart from the general rowdiness of the MPs, the monks had to cope not only with vacating the hall when MPs needed it, but also to the consequences of up to 300 MPs needing to wash their hands and use the latrines. The sharing of the hall was not a marriage made in Heaven. It was mainly used when Westminster Hall or other parts of the Palace of Westminster were unavailable or unsuitable.

*The surviving wall of the dining hall in the garden of Westminster school*

Ashburnham House, now part of Westminster School. Part of it can be seen from a window in the upstairs section of the Abbey's Cellarium Café which is open to the public.

The new permanent home lasted for nearly 300 years until the great fire of 1834 which destroyed nearly all of the old palace including St Stephen's Chapel (but the crypt of St Mary Undercroft immediately underneath escaped serious damage). The Chapel was reconstructed in the same style as before by Charles Barry, the architect of the new Parliament building. The revamped building, called St Stephen's Hall, is now the entrance for public visits to Parliament For much of its life, the Chapel, which dates back to 1365, together with the associated St Stephen's College, were at the centre of not just religion but political life as well. This was because the canons who lived there were diplomats and administrators as well as ministers of religion. MPs weren't the only ones involved with politics.

It is clear that individual countries are adept at interpreting their parliamentary history in a nationalistic way and England is no exception, but the claim that England is the mother of parliaments is difficult to refute. Mothers have children and as a result of Britain's history of colonialism, the legacy of the English Parliament is evident in the way medieval common law has influenced the legal systems of Canada, Australia, India and

*The reconstructed St Stephen's Chapel, now the public entrance to Parliament*

the West Indies and concepts like parliamentary sovereignty and judicial independence can be seen in many countries. At the time of writing, the American system was in a state of flux, but as one US law firm put it: "the relationship between English law and American law is akin to a river that has branched off from its primary source. While they flow separately, their shared origin is undeniable".

# 12: St Stephen's, where Church and politics came together

The stunning chapel of St Mary Undercroft and the equally stunning cloisters surrounding it (below) are all that remain of the medieval Palace of Westminster, apart from the Jewel Tower on the opposite side of Old Palace Yard. Sadly, only the Jewel Tower is open to the public today as the cloisters are used by MPs for parliamentary business and the undercroft is deemed too small to accommodate regular visitors. Originally, they were all part of St Stephen's Chapel and its associated institution, St Stephen's College.

St Mary's is the undercroft of St Stephen's Chapel, described by the parliamentary website as "the forgotten heart of the Palace of Westminster". They should know. For centuries after it was finally finished in 1365, the Chapel, together with St Stephen's College, were at the centre not just of religion but of political life as well. This was because the canons who lived there were diplomats and administrators, as well as ministers of religion. After the Reformation around 1548, the newly secularised building was handed over

*The historic Chapel of St Mary Undercroft (UK Parliament / Estates Archive)*

to MPs as their first permanent home. That lasted until the Great Fire of 1834 when it was completely destroyed (but not the Undercroft). The Chapel is now called St Stephen's Hall and is the entrance for public visits to Parliament.

It all began in 1248 when King Henry lll (1207-1272) was in Paris at the consecration of the mind-bogglingly beautiful stained glass masterpiece known as Sainte Chappelle. English Kings didn't like to be outdone by other monarchs, especially not if they were French. Henry's reaction was immediate. He wanted a Sainte Chappelle of his own at his palace at Westminster. As it turned out, Sainte Chapelle influenced Henry's extensive reconstruction of Westminster Abbey but St Stephen's itself was actually started later on by Edward I and completed in fits and starts during the reigns of Edward II and Edward III. It is regarded as one of the great building projects of the Middle Ages, but because of the stop/start nature of its construction it took over 70 years before it was finally completed in 1365. (In case of interest, the 1851 Crystal Palace, the largest building in the world at the time, constructed of cast iron and glass, took a mere nine months to build).

St Stephen's Chapel consisted of an upper building which was originally a chapel of the Royal Family, and a lower part known as St Mary Undercroft which was started separately and used by the court and royal household. The Undercroft was formally completed in 1297 some 50 years earlier than the Upper Chapel. The College was a religious institution within the Chapel which was built to pray for dead members of the royal family, but it also played a significant role in the political and administrative life of Old Westminster.

*Medieval survivor - Cloister Court west walk: (UK Parliament / Estates Archive)*

Of these institutions, the stunning St Mary Undercroft is particularly interesting because, despite all the fires and religious and political upheavals, it is still there with surrounding cloisters, largely in pristine condition. It was started by Edward I in 1297 and added to by Edward II and Edward III until finally completed in 1365. It was called an undercroft rather than a crypt because it has windows on one side so wasn't completely enclosed. After the Reformation, the Upper Chapel, which had been used by the Royal Family, was deemed surplus to requirements because of its Popish heritage and was handed over to the House of Commons. It was destroyed during the Great Fire of 1834, but was faithfully reconstructed to become today's St Stephen's Hall, the public entrance to Parliament.

The unsavory conditions of the cloisters led the former Labour Home Secretary Jack Straw to describe the area as a Gothic slum. Apart from the Jewel Tower and Westminster Hall (the latter not part of the old royal palace) the cloisters and the undercroft are the only surviving remnants of the old Palace which lasted from the 11th century until Henry VIII moved the whole shebang up the road to Whitehall after the fire of 1512.

*Not yet open to the public - Cloister Court (Parliament / Estates Archive)*

It is reckoned that 80% of the undercroft is more or less original and the rest modernised.

There has been a lot of research in recent years into St Stephen's College, a collegiate institution linked to the Chapel (built 50 years later) including a virtual reproduction of it which can be seen at

https://www.virtualststephens.org.uk/explore

For seven centuries, St Stephen's was at the centre of the political and religious life of the nation. The height of its political influence was during its long association with the upwardly mobile Cardinal Wolsey. Wolsey was more associated with St Stephen's College than St Stephen's Chapel. He served as the dean of St Stephen's College from 1512 to 1514, during which time he played a role in its development, including the construction of the cloisters. His coat of arms can be seen as a "boss" in the ceiling of the east walk of the cloister.

According to historian Elizabeth Biggs, Wolsey used the opportunity to reward his faithful priests and retinue whilst also placing his own followers in the royal administration. In 1511, Wolsey's unofficial brother-in-law Thomas Larke was made a cannon. Larke's sister Joan was Wolsey's mistress and the mother of his son Thomas Winter who also appears as a cannon until 1529, when he was pushed out after his father's downfall when Wolsey failed to get an annulment of Henry VIII's marriage to Catherine of Aragon. John Veysey, Richard Samson and Thomas Thirlby (remembered today by Thirlby Road off Victoria Street) also owed their advancement to Wolsey.

After the Reformation, St Stephen's was handed over to the emerging House of Commons as their first permanent home where MPs sat until the Great Fire of 1834 when it was redesigned by Charles Barry as St Stephen's Hall. It is now the public entrance into Parliament.

# 13: King Cnut - did he or didn't he?

*Canute giving his courtiers a physics lesson (1848 R E Pine public domain)*

King Canute - or Cnut - is best known as the monarch who may, or may not, have tried to hold back the oncoming waves on a beach somewhere or other. Less well known is that he was the most successful of four Danish kings who ruled England and was the first king to build a palace on Thorney Island. Part of the evidence for this is that his son Harold Harefoot - who was regent of England from 1035 to 1037 and King of the English from 1037 to 1040 - was buried in the Abbey, albeit briefly, which makes it likely that Cnut had been living in a palace there.

Not many people strolling from Parliament Square towards Millbank realise that they are likely walking over the remains of the palace of Canute.

*Medieval impression depicting Edmund Ironside (left) and Canute (right).*

For the next 500 years, Thorney Island was the royal palace of kings and queens. It was usually their main residence, until the fire of 1512 when Henry VIII, whose favourite dwelling it apparently was, had to move out while he built a much bigger palace in what is today's Whitehall.

Monarchs didn't usually spend much time at their London abodes as they had so many other mansions and palaces to go to. This was particularly true of Cnut as England wasn't the only country he was monarch of. He became King of England in December 1016, King of Denmark from 1018, and King of Norway from 1028, until his death in 1035.

Cnut became King of England by invasion. He was the son of a ruthless Viking, the unforgettably named Sweyn Forkbeard, the King of Denmark who had previously conquered and ruled England for less than five weeks, a record shorter even than Liz Truss who was Prime Minister from September to October 2022.

After Sweyn's death in February 1014, aged 50,

an inexperienced Cnut invaded England, but failed to retain his father's conquered lands. A year later he returned to England with a huge fleet. Even so, it took more than a year of brutal warfare before Cnut, helped by mercenaries, seized control of England.

When the English King Æthelred died in 1016, his son Edmund Ironside led the defence against Cnut's Danes. They both fought battles across the south of England leading to a final one in Essex, probably at Ashingdon, where Cnut's Danes were victorious with many killed on the English side. The Anglo-Saxon Chronicle noted that "all the best of the English nation" were slain.

After the battle, Edmund and Cnut agreed to make peace, dividing the kingdom between them. Edmund died just six weeks later in possibly controversial circumstances. Cnut was left as sole King of England and turned, surprisingly, into something like a model ruler. He brought stability to a country that had been suffering from perpetual raids by Vikings from across the North Sea. He turned the country into an integrated state which made it easier to collect taxes to fund any wars. This was such a successful formula that Cnut applied it to his native Denmark and other countries under his rule.

Success in war appeared to make Cnut a more gentle and religious character, at least when had seen off or executed rival nobles. It was maybe part of this newfound gentility that persuaded Cnut - if of course the story is true - to assemble his courtiers to see whether he could stem the waves. The main source for this story was Henry of Huntingdon who in the 12th century quoted it as an example of Cnut's "graceful and magnificent behaviour".

According to Huntingdon, Canute set his throne by the sea shore and "commanded the incoming tide to halt and not wet his feet and robes". Yet "continuing to rise as usual (the tide) dashed over his feet and legs without respect to his royal person". Then the King leapt backwards, saying: "Let all men know how empty and worthless is the power of kings, for there is none worthy of the name, but He whom heaven, earth, and sea obey by eternal laws." He then hung his gold crown on a crucifix, and never wore it again.

Cnut's purpose was not, as many in the past have believed, to command the waves to go back but to prove that he was a mere mortal and could not do such a thing. Only God could do that. This can be interpreted as displaying Cnut's modesty or, alternatively, his pride as he may be hinting that as a King his powers were second only to that of God.

The site of the episode is often identified as Thorney Island (Westminster), where Canute set up a royal palace. There is, however, another Thorney Island, a small peninsula within Chichester harbour with a rival claim and, confusingly, a sign on Canute Road in Southampton's city centre which reads, "Near

*Cnut enthroned*

this spot, AD 1028 Canute reproved his courtiers". Bosham in West Sussex also claims to be the site of this episode, as does Gainsborough in Lincolnshire. As Gainsborough is inland, if the story is true, then Canute would have been trying to turn back the tidal bore known as the Aegir, a name borrowed from Norse mythology. Another tradition places this episode on the north coast of the Wirral, which at the time was part of Mercia. The fact that Huntingdon mentions that the incident happened by the sea shore may rule out Westminster in some eyes, but in those days the Thames was both tidal and much wider than it is today. Who knows? Maybe it was just an early example of fake news proving that fiction is so often more powerful than fact.

# 14: Drama above the bookshop

*The Abbey bookshop beneath the Jerusalem Chamber and ancient hall*

Not many people going into the Abbey bookshop bother to look at the stone wall above. It is no ordinary stone wall. Built in the 14th century mainly of Kentish ragstone, it is actually part of two buildings dripping with history either side of the narrow vertical column which divides the top of the Jerusalem Chamber on the left from the longer College Hall on the right. They are part of the Abbot's dwelling known as Cheyneygates (from the French chene meaning oak). It is probably the longest continuously occupied home in London, if not in the rest of the country as well. It was here that the future King Edward V, later one of the Princes in the Tower, was born to the Queen, Elizabeth Woodville, when she claimed sanctuary in 1470 when Edward IV was exiled abroad. It was where she moved in 1483

a second time, seeking sanctuary after the death of Edward IV and was persuaded to let her younger son Richard join his brother in the Tower of London.

The longer wall on the right is the top of one side of College Hall, currently used as a dining hall for King's Scholars of Westminster School, but in medieval times was where Elizabeth I used to come to witness pupils performing their traditional play in Latin and is also where Elizabeth Woodville spent much of her second stay in sanctuary. It is said to be one of the finest examples of a medieval refectory and its long tables made of chestnut wood were supposedly made from a wrecked vessel captured during the Spanish Armada.

Next door is one end of the historic Jerusalem Chamber. The most dramatic event that took place there was the death of Henry IV, but the most influential was the signing off of the King James Bible. You don't have to be a believer to appreciate the wonder of this event.

The Jerusalem Chamber was one of three places - Oxford, Cambridge and Westminster - where the King James (KJ) Bible was compiled, and it was the actual room in which it was eventually signed off in 1611. This was a book written by committees, surely, you might think, a certain recipe for failure. Yet it turned out to be one of the most influential - and beautifully written - books ever produced, having sold over 5 billion copies worldwide in its various versions. The Harry Potter series has notched up a mere 500 million copies (though still one of the all-time best selling books).

Melvin Bragg, the author and presenter, in his book The Adventure of English, says it became "the most influential book that there has ever been in the history of language, English, or any other". No book has sold more copies than the King James Bible all over the world.

Actuallly, the KJ Bible was very heavily based on William Tyndale's earlier bible which had been banned among other things because - horror of horrors - it was written in English not Latin so interpretation would no longer be

*The Jerusalem Chamber today*

the preserve of monks and priests, but available to ordinary people to make their own minds up.

Tyndale translated key parts of the Bible from Greek and Hebrew into English to fulfill his ambition to make the Bible accessible to ordinary people so that even a "boy who driveth the plow" would be able to read the Scriptures.

In 1530 Sir Thomas Moore, author of the idealised world, Utopia, disagreed. He had complained about the disgrace of the Bible being in English "in the language of ploughboys". Despite this, the KJ Bible sold 5bn copies to ploughboys and all.

But whose bible was it? An astonishing amount of Tyndale's earlier version was retained in the KJ Bible. A paper by Jon Nielson and Royal Akousen claims that "for the New Testament, Tyndale's contribution is about 84 per cent of the text, while in the Old

Testament about 76 per cent of his words have been retained". This is not just plagiarism, but plagiarism on an industrial scale.

And what happened to William Tyndale? Did he get any royalties? No, he was at the time on the wrong side of the Reformation. He was convicted of heresy in 1536 and executed by strangulation before his body was burnt at the stake in Brabant near Brussels. But they didn't kill his reputation. In 2002, Tyndale came 26th in the BBC's poll of the 100 greatest Britons.

# 15: The unique story of Poets' Corner

A unique treasure of Westminster Abbey is Poets' Corner, where Britain's literary greatness is sanctified. I still feel a mild buzz whenever I visit it, but I sometimes wonder how many people in this country have actually heard about the space let alone know the three poets whose burial in the Abbey gave rise to it.

There are two ways of looking at Poets' Corner: one is what is there and the other is what is not there. What is not there, let's face it, is any representation of half of the population. For well over 400 years not a single female poet or playwright has been buried in this hallowed spot (though there are a few memorials such as to Fanny Burney), a sobering reminder of the historic dominance of the male, not least ecclesiastical, over our culture.

It took three men to establish it as a "corner" for poets. Geoffrey Chaucer, author of the Canterbury Tales, was the first to be buried in the south transept of the Abbey in 1400. However, this was not because of his poetic genius but because of his day job - he was Clerk of the King's Works. He was later moved to his present position in 1556 over 150 years later, probably because Queen "Bloody" Mary (who reigned from 1553 to 1558) wanted to restore a bit of Catholicism to the Abbey after the rigid Protestantism of her predecessor Edward VI, the son of Henry VIII.

Chaucer is still one of Britain's greatest writers. His "Canterbury Tales" hasn't been out of print for approaching 600 years though if you are in Poets' Corner today it is noticeable that practically all the visitors have their backs to his ancient grave with eyes only for the numerous memorial slabs on the floor in front with more familiar names such as Tennyson, Henry James, T S Eliot and Robert Browning.

However, one poetic burial doesn't make a grouping. Edmund Spenser, author of The Faerie Queene, dedicated to Elizabeth I, was the second person to be buried in what was at the time a little used space in the Abbey. Some of his poems such as Prothalamion were so rammed into me at grammar school - with punishment if you forgot - that I can still remember them today ("Calm was the day

*Poets' Corner without visitors. Left to right Chaucer, Drayton, Spenser*

and through the trembling air sweet breathing Zephyrus did softly play," etc.)

What we didn't learn at school was that this wonderful lyrical poet - writer of lines like "Sweet Thames run softly till I end my song" - also had a day job. He had been Secretary to Lord Grey, Lord Deputy of Ireland, where he favoured a scorched earth policy to defeat the rebels who eventually succeeded in expelling him from his dwelling and plundered his goods. He returned to England a poor man. He died shortly afterwards and was buried near his hero Chaucer.

The third of the early occupants

*How not to look at Chaucer's grave*

of Poets' Corner was Michael Drayton, whose profile could easily have been mistaken for that of Shakespeare: born and bred in Warwickshire, went to London, a prolific poet, author or part-author of over 20 plays and part owner of a playhouse. Of the portraits of Drayton and Shakespeare that normally hang in the National Portrait Gallery, it is Drayton who is wearing the laurels. Few major poets have been forgotten so quickly.

What is regarded as Drayton's magnum opus, Poly-Olbion, is one of the most extraordinary poems in the English language. That is partly because of its length (15,000 lines in iambic pentameter), partly because of how long it took to write (30 years), and partly because of the subject matter. It is a topographical

epic about the history of England and Wales, which E M Forster called an "incomparable poem". It may be about to get a reappraisal. Exeter University has been involved in a major study of Poly-Olbion, not yet published at the time of writing.

On 23rd December 1631, Drayton died at his Fleet Street home almost penniless, his form of pastoral poetry having gone out of fashion. Yet he was so highly regarded by his contemporaries that, according to the antiquary William Fulman: "The Gentlemen of the Four Innes of Court and others of note about the Town, attended his body to Westminster."

Drayton is perhaps best known today by the claim that it was after a heavy drinking session in a

Stratford-upon-Avon tavern in 1616 with Ben Jonson and Shakespeare that the latter contracted an illness and died. Experts have tended to disbelieve this tale as it was based on a claim by a local clergyman over 30 years after Shakespeare's death. I used to find that disbelief credible, but now that I'm at an age when I can more easily remember what happened 40 years previously that a few minutes ago I am not so sure.

It is a sobering fact that at least two of the three founding writers in Poets' Corner - Drayton and Spenser - died in poverty only to be given what seemed like State funerals on their deaths. It is also possible, but not yet proven, that Chaucer, burdened by unpaid debts, also died in poverty. Even more sobering is the likelihood that nearly all of the visitors to the Abbey and Poets' Corner - mainly from abroad - have never heard of Drayton or Spenser and many of them probably haven't heard of Chaucer either despite the fact that The Canterbury Tales hasn't been out of print for well over 500 years. The times they are a' changing. This does nothing to alter the fact that there always seems to be a bit of magic in the air as visitors become imbued at least temporarily in the thrall of poesy in the much expanded Poets' Corner.

Thomas A Prendergast in his scholarly history of Poets' Corner, Poetical Dust, says that it was only after Lady Anne Clifford, Countess of Dorset, erected monuments to both Edmund Spenser in 1620 and to Michael Drayton in1631, that Poets' Corner became somewhere special. This, he suggests, makes her "the godmother of the modern notion of Poets Corner". What Anne Clifford would have made of the fact that nearly 400 years after she helped to establish it there are still no women buried at Poets' Corner, can only be guessed at.

Once you become aware of the absence of women at Poets' Corner it conjures up their presence in an

*Shakespeare and Michael Drayton (left, wearing the laurel crown) in the National Portrait Gallery.*

ethereal way, a kind of virtual monument, defined by their absence. This also applies to one man who isn't buried there, William Shakespeare. He has a memorial but his body remains buried in his local church Holy Trinity in Stratford-upon-Avon, despite various unsuccessful attempts to move it to Westminster.

It clearly takes something away from the grandeur of Poets' Corner that there are no women buried there and our only poet/playwright with global recognition, Shakespeare, is buried elsewhere, but it doesn't seem to worry the huge number of visitors, well over 90% from abroad, who pass through it each day.

# 16: The women who didn't qualify for Poets' Corner

*Men's club - Poets' corner before the crowds arrive*

who might have qualified for Poets' Corner, summed up the situation neatly:

"I am obnoxious to each carping tongue

Who says my hand a needle better fits.

A Poet's Pen all scorn I should thus wrong,

For such despite they cast on female wits.

If what I do prove well, it won't advance,

They'll say it's stol'n, or melse it was by chance."

Poets' Corner is one of the most exclusive male preserves in the country. In recent years a number of memorial plaques for female poets have been created, but no woman has been buried there since it was started with the tomb of Geoffrey Chaucer at the start of the 15th century. It is not that there were no worthy female candidates, but none could breach the prejudices of the 17th century when male decision makers - including the Dean and Chapter of Westminster Abbey - didn't even stop to think whether women could be considered as serious poets.

Anne Bradstreet, who was one of a number of women

Anne was an accomplished scholar who emigrated to the American colonies around 1630, aged 16, with her wealthy Northampton Puritan family. She is recognised as an accomplished poet as well as being the mother of eight children. She was the first person to be recognised as a published poet in America. There is no recognition of her in Westminster Abbey, but a Bradstreet Gate was erected in 1997 at Harvard University of which her father was one of the founders.

The absence of women at Poets' Corner is bizarre because it was a woman, Lady Anne Clifford, Countess of Dorset, who was instrumental in the early

*Anne Bradstreet*

Aphra was a star of Restoration drama during the reign of Charles II. She wrote poetry and 18 successful plays which was more than any male dramatist at the time, with the possible exception of John Dryden. She was held in esteem by her peers but not long after sank almost without trace for centuries. This was partly because Restoration drama fell out of fashion and partly because she wrote in a bawdy fashion which was tolerated for men - such as the Earl of Rochester - but later not thought a fit occupation for a woman.

In recent years she has made a comeback partly due to Virginia Woolf's famous exhortation on her tomb, that "all women together ought to let flowers fall".

Which is what happened in the Summer of 2021, when pupils from Urswick School in Hackney laid flowers on her grave with personal messages after they had given a performance of some of Aphra's work in the hallowed atmosphere of nearby Poets' Corner. I was delighted to be part of the audience

establishment of the corner as a special place. Both the second and third occupants of the space, Edmund Spenser and Michael Drayton (who is hardly known at all these days), were sponsored by the Countess. She was also a friend of Amelia Lanier, now recognised as a proto-feminist and the first woman in England to have published a collection of her own poetry. She even dared to think that maybe Adam tempted Eve in the Garden of Eden and not the other way around.

Some people think Amelia was the Dark Lady of Shakespeare's sonnets. Others that she actually wrote the works of Shakespeare, but let that pass. She lived for a key part of her life a stone's throw away from Poets' Corner in Longditch (today's Storey's Gate). She would certainly have been a candidate for Poets' Corner in an open contest.

One woman who nearly made it, at least geographically, was Aphra Behn, poet and playwright, who is buried literally a few yards away in the East Cloister of the Abbey. Only a stone wall - and a glass ceiling - have kept her out.

**54**

*Dropping flowers on Aphra Benn's tomb*

nowadays pored over for signs of deep insights. Her observations about natural science are today highly thought of. Her book, The Blazing World, is thought to be the first work of science fiction by a woman and a pioneer of the genre itself.

Lucy Hutchinson (1620–1681) was a poet and translator who emerged from almost total anonymity in her own time to being considered a formidable author in her own right and a pioneering writer in English literary history. She was the first person to translate the text of Lucretius's De Rerum Natura (On the Nature of Things) into heroic couplets and for writing Order and Disorder, also in heroic couplets. Often seen as a parallel version of Milton's Paradise Lost from a female perspective, it has some claim to be the first epic poem written by an English woman. Germaine Greer acknowledges Hutchinson as "a serious writer who dared to undertake ambitious works on the largest scale" and calls her "a hero."

Another woman of literary note in the 17th century was Katherine (or Catherine) Philips (1632-1664) who was an Anglo-Welsh poet, playwright, a woman of letters and the translator of Pompey by the French playwright Pierre Corneille. Editions of her poetry published after her death were well received and she was highly regarded by later writers, including John Dryden and Keats.

These are but a few examples of women poets in the 17th century whose achievements are all the more impressive because they had to overcome not only the bias against women writers, but often also the time-consuming demands of married life. It is now unlikely that any women poets will be buried in the traditional way in the Abbey as pressure of space means almost all burials these days - such as those of Stephen Hawking - are of cremated remains.

along with others from London Historians. Aphra was from a humble background, but became an icon and role model. She is still a talking point among feminists, partly because she dealt with gender mixing themes and was a proud libertine at a time when it was fashionable among men. She didn't seem to believe in a God, yet she dedicated part of a play to the staunchly Catholic James II before he did a moonlight flit out of the country.

Aphra was probably the first woman to earn her living from writing, even though she was always short of money. Nell Gwynn appeared in one of her plays as did Anne Bracegirdle, an esteemed actress of the time (in The Widow Ranter in 1689). Anne is buried next to Aphra in the East Cloister.

Also qualified for Poets' Corner was the astonishing Margaret Cavendish (details chapter 41) to whom history until recently has been wantonly unkind. The Duchess was a prolific author. She produced ten volumes of what have been described as "learned trifles and fantastic verses". Cavendish was an early feminist whose poems, plays and literary critiques are

# 17: Three extraordinary 18th century black men of letters

Thorney Island has special links with several extraordinary 18th century writers of African descent who escaped from a background of slavery to become best-selling authors and leading abolitionists. While they were campaigning, Britain was still heavily engaged in the international slave trade and also fighting America and its allies, France and Spain, in the American War of Independence.

The pioneers were Ignatius Sancho (1729-1780) and his wife Anne; Olaudau Equiano (1745-1797) who lived for a while on Thorney Island, and Ottobah Cugoano (1757-1791) who lived close by, overlooking St James's Park. There is also a fourth, Francis Williams, whose extraordinary success has only recently emerged and is still being investigated. At the time of writing it was not known where he spent most of his time in London, though he may have lodged nearby. What is known is that the Duke of Montagu who mentored Sancho had a London home in the Thames near Thorney Island and it is claimed

Sancho's plaque with his wife Ann

Equiano's baptismal plaque in St Margaret's Church

he helped Williams to go to Cambridge. There is no concrete evidence of this, but it could be that the record was either lost or erased. Williams must have got his considerable scientific knowledge from somewhere.

Such success would have been highly unusual for anyone from a penniless white background at a time of widespread illiteracy. For it to happen to uneducated black people who emerged from a background of slavery and didn't speak the language when they arrived, is genuinely amazing. There are still lessons to be learned today.

They lived in a variety of places in London, but all three had special ties with this part of Westminster. St Margaret's Church, which is so close to Westminster Abbey that from a short distance it looks part of it, was where Equiano was baptised and Sancho married. Sancho's children were baptised there. He himself is buried with his family in Christchurch Gardens in Palmer Street near the Albert pub which was then part of the burial ground of St Margaret's.

Black history also has another little known link with Thorney Island. James Edward Oglethorpe, a Tory politician who lived in Old Palace Yard close to Westminster Hall, founded the colony of Georgia in 1731 where he introduced a ban on slavery. It faded after his departure from Georgia, but it remains an initiative long in advance of the success of English abolitionists towards the end of the century led by people like William Wilberforce (who lived in Old Palace Yard on the other side of the road to Oglethorpe).

It is a curious fact that Sancho, Equiano and Cugoano (who worked in the studio of Richard Crosway overlooking St James's Park) adopted the religion of their oppressors, but then used it to bang them to rights. In the preface to his book Cugoano explains why when he quotes the bible stating "he that stealeth a man and selleth him… then that thief shall die."

Equiano recalls in his book how shortly after his arrival in London following a trip abroad with his slave master, Captain Pascal, he was sent to wait upon two sisters called the Miss Guerins in Greenwich. They had treated him with great kindness when he was there before and sent him to school.

He recalled that "while attending these ladies, their servants told me I could not go to Heaven unless I was baptised. This made me very uneasy; for I had now some faint idea of a future state: accordingly I communicated my anxiety to the eldest Miss Guerin, with whom I had become a favourite, and pressed her to have me baptised; when to my great joy she told me I should. I was baptised in St. Margaret's church, Westminster, in February 1759".

He added: "I used to attend these ladies about the town, in which service I was extremely happy; as I had thus many opportunities of seeing London, which I desired of all things. I was sometimes, however, with my master at his rendezvous-house, at the foot of Westminster-bridge. Here I used to enjoy myself by playing about the bridge stairs, and often in the watermen's wherries, with other boys.

*Ignatius Sancho by Gainsborough*

On one of these occasions there was another boy with me in a wherry, and we went out into the current of the river: while we were there two more stout boys came to us in another wherry, and, abusing us for taking the boat, desired me to get into the other wherry-boat. Accordingly I went to get out of the wherry I was in; but just as I had got one of my feet into the other boat the boys shoved it off, so that I fell into the Thames; and, not being able to swim, I should unavoidably have been drowned, but for the assistance of some watermen who providentially came to my relief." If it had not been for such providence with the waters lapping Thorney Island, a man who later became one of the leading protagonists of abolition would have been denied to us.

Charles Ignatius Sancho, to give him his full name, lived for a time in Canon Row before moving across today's Whitehall to nearby (King) Charles Street. He was employed by the aristocratic Montagu family led by the Duke of Montagu, and his successor George Brudenell who became Duke Montagu of the second creation. The Montagus had numerous homes spread around England and Scotland including Greenwich and Richmond, but their main London abode was a Thames-side mansion in the Privy Garden a short stroll from Canon Row and (King) Charles Street. When a worsening outbreak of gout made it impossible for Sancho to work as a butler, Mary, the Duchess of Montagu, helped to set him up with a grocery shop in (King) Charles Street where the Foreign Office is today. She left him seventy pounds in her will, and an annuity of thirty pounds.

Ownership of the shop gave Sancho a property qualification to vote. He was one of the first known black people in Britain to vote in an election. He cast his vote for Charles James Fox, a fellow abolitionist with whom he was friendly.

*An advert for tobacco sold by Sancho in his shop.*

Sancho, who was successful as a writer, composer and celebrity, was feted by Dr Johnson, painted by Gainsborough, and was a correspondent of Laurence Sterne (author of the hugely influential novel, The Life and Opinions of Tristram Shandy, Gentleman) whom he actively encouraged to campaign against slavery. Sancho's shop which, ironically, sold some of the products of slavery such as tobacco and sugar (there wasn't much in the way of alternatives, such was the reach of slavery) was something of a social hub with painters, sculptors and politicians dropping by for a chat as well as a few purchases.

Sancho's stay on Thorney Island was dramatically reconstructed in October, 2023 (photo above) when the celebrated black actor Paterson Joseph, dressed in a similar garb to what Sancho was wearing when he was painted by Gainsborough, seemingly entered the mind and soul of Sancho as he entertained an audience to scenes from Sancho's life. This was based on his book, The Secret Diaries of Charles Ignatius Sancho .

The reenactment took place in the same St Margaret's Church, where Sancho was married, which has barely changed from the original. As Paterson walked up and down the aisle he was literally walking in the footsteps of Sancho when he married his beloved bride, Anne. Westminster Abbey completed the reality of the occasion by displaying the actual marriage and baptismal documents of Sancho's family at the back of the church.

Sancho's letters (published after his death), and Equiano's autobiography both became best-sellers subscribed to by a dizzy list of the great and the good that might have stepped out of Debrett's. The 1,200 subscribers to Sancho's book included leading dukes, earls and duchesses, the Prime Minister, Lord North, and the historian Edward Gibbon, author of The Decline and Fall of the Roman Empire.

A surprising number of the subscribers, such as William Beckford, were actually slave owners. Whether this was part of their journey towards abolition, mere curiosity, or an example of`English hypocrisy is a moot point.

In one of his final letters, Sancho described the Gordon Riots that started after Lord Gordon, an eccentric Scottish peer, presented a peaceful petition to Parliament, a few hundred yards from Sancho's shop. He was protesting about the Government's plans to make it easier for Roman Catholics to join the army. Ironically, many already had joined, thanks to a shortage of people willing to enlist.

Gordon progressed to Parliament with the petition after a meeting on Kennington Common attended by an estimated 60,000 people. What started off as a religious movement led by Gordon against quite minor relaxations of the strict rules stopping Roman Catholics from taking part in public life, exploded into the worst disturbances London had witnessed since

*The Gordon Riots*

the Peasants' Revolt in 1381. Thorney Island and the rest of central London had seen nothing like it.

From nearby King Charles Street where he lived and near where the riots started, Sancho gave a blow-by-blow report of what he saw happening, referring to the "maddest people that the maddest times were ever plagued with". He added: "Government is sunk in lethargic stupor—anarchy reigns . . . the Fleet prison, the Marshalsea, King's-Bench, both Compeers (small debtors' prisons), Clerkenwell and Tothill Fields, with Newgate are all flung open and 300 felons from thence only let loose upon the world".

Equiano's book, a riveting blow-by-blow account of his experience of slavery, was also a dizzying success, attracting over 300 subscribers including the Prince of Wales, the Duke of York, Josua Wedgwood, Granville Sharp, the Duke of Montagu, William Sancho (the son of Ignatius Sancho), and Ottobah Cugoano, the active abolitionist operating from Richard Cosway's studio backing on to St James's Park.

Cugoano knew Equiano, who helped him write his book but, curiously, we don't know whether Sancho and Equiano ever met even though they lived close

to each other for a short period. Sancho was living in Canon Row when Equiano purchased his freedom and Sancho married Ann in St Margaret's Church in 1758 a year before Equiano was baptised there aged 12. If they ever saw each other they would certainly have had lots to talk about, but whether they did or not will have to await more research perhaps even the discovery of more letters. Meanwhile both of them have plaques in St Margaret's Church cementing their links with Thorney Island.

The success of Sancho and Equiano was likely due to their own determination and because both of them were helped by mentors. Cugoano's memoirs, which also attracted a long list of subscribers are sometimes - rather bizarrely - criticised for their lapses in grammar, a curious criticism of someone who emerged from slavery to write an acclaimed denunciation of slavery in a second language. Cugoano was the most radical of the abolitionists as he campaigned not just for the abolition of the international trade in slaves but for the abolition of slavery itself.

Cugoano also raised the delicate question of the layers of guilt in the slave trade. He admitted: 'I must own, to the shame of my own countrymen, that I was first kid-napped and betrayed by some of my own complexion, who were the first cause of my exile and slavery; but if there were no buyers there would be no sellers". He knew that some of the Africans in his country kept slaves but claimed "they were well-fed, and good care taken of them".

At the time, these memoirs were promoted as examples of what black people could achieve if only they were given the chance, a proposition that still rings urgently true today.

# 18: The haunting presence of Shakespeare on Thorney Island

On Monday, 11th May 1612, William Shakespeare visited Thorney Island though he probably wouldn't have known it by that name. This was the day he was summoned to the Court of Requests - a sort of small claims court - in the White Chamber adjacent to Westminster Hall. He gave evidence in a dispute between two inhabitants of a house in Silver Street, Cripplegate, where he was a lodger. It was about the time he was writing one of his last plays - The Tempest - so he may have had to take time off.

This was a small case for the Court of Requests, but a bigger one for Shakespeare scholars. The house in Silver Street is the only place we know for certain that Shakespeare actually lived in. Nothing of it remains, but its location is in an underground car park in London Wall.

Fig 17: The fireplace in the Jerusalem Chamber where Henry IV died in Shakespeare's play and in real life

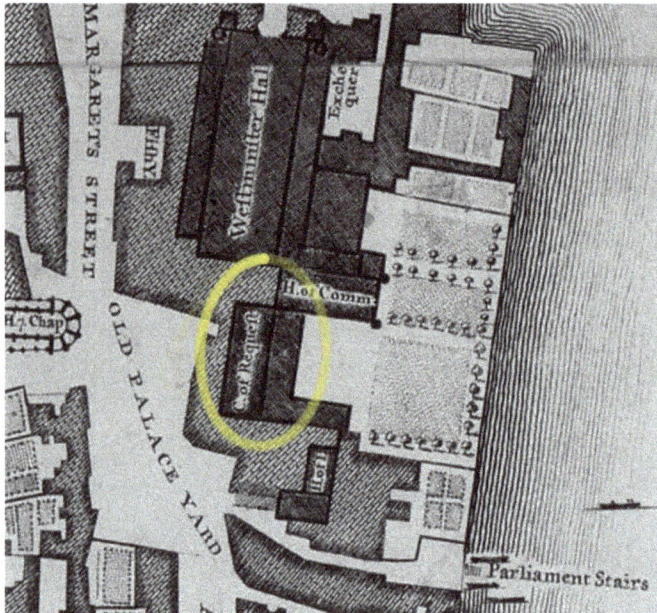

*The Court of Requests where Shakespeare spoke*

been performed at Court were The Comedy of Errors, Measure for Measure, Love's Labours Lost, Othello, the Merry Wives of Windsor and The Tempest all of which would have probably needed the presence of the author. The Cockpit on the other side of the road was sometimes used for theatrical performances especially by the young Prince of Wales.

Shakespeare occasionally inserted local references into his plays as in Henry VIII, which he jointly wrote with John Fletcher. When the First Gent rebukes his colleague for wrongly calling Cardinal Wolsey's former palace "York Place", he says:

"For since the Cardinal fell, that title's lost:
tis now the King's and called Whitehall."

Most of his plays took place abroad, but several were actually located on Thorney Island and have affected our view of history. Two of them, Richard III and Henry IV (part 2) happened in different parts of the rooms of the Dean of Westminster Abbey called Cheynegates, both of which can be viewed today, at least from the outside.

In Henry IV (part 2), Shakespeare set a vital scene in the Jerusalem Chamber (fig 17) where Henry IV was dying and where the future Henry V comes in and, wrongly thinking his father was dead, tries on the crown which, whether true or false, has governed the way we think of it ever since. The scene took place by the same fireplace as in the recent photo (above) taken in the Jerusalem Chamber.

In Shakespeare's Richard III - as happened in real life - the Queen of England, Elizabeth Woodville, who had taken refuge in the Sanctuary of the Abbey at Cheynegates, was persuaded to let her son Richard leave the Abbey, where they had both claimed

During the course of the case, Shakespeare had to make a statement which was taken down by a clerk for him to sign. As Charles Nicholl points out in his splendid book, The Lodger, this event close to Westminster Hall is the only time that Shakespeare's actual spoken words were recorded, as opposed to the thousands of lines he had written. His scrawly signature at the bottom was the first he had made though five others were found subsequently. The words he uttered were rather banal. He didn't speak, as he often wrote, in iambic pentameters.

Shakespeare left more than fleeting footprints on Thorney Island. His troupe performed nearly 200 times at court, which mainly meant the grand hall in Whitehall, a stone's throw from the core of Thorney Island, just behind today's Banqueting House.

It is highly likely that Shakespeare would have attended rehearsals and performances even if he was not acting in them. Among the plays known to have

62

Sanctuary (freedom from arrest) in order to join his brother, the future Edward V, in the Tower of London.

In Shakespeare's play, supported by the opinion of Sir Thomas More, the Princes were murdered on the orders of Richard III in order to block their rival claims to the succession. That sounds feasible and has been repeated in books and taught in schools around the world ever since. It is an interesting case of Shakespeare not only recording history, but shaping the way we think about it.

But is Shakespeare's version true?

A team led by Phillipa Langley - in a Channel 4 documentary in November 2023 - strongly argued, apparently with authenticated documents from Continental archives, that the Princes escaped from the Tower of London to Europe and returned to England with armed support under the disguises of Lambert Simnel as the deposed Edward V, elder son of King Edward IV, and four years later Perkin Warbeck claiming to be Richard, Duke of York, the second son of Edward IV. If true, Richard would have had a rightful claim to the throne if his elder brother had died, as was likely, during his failed rebellion.

Phillipa Langley's claims have been taken seriously because of her earlier success in finding the remains of Richard III in a Leicester car park.

There has, of course, always been something enigmatic about Shakespeare. After all, over 400 years after his death, experts are still arguing about whether he actually wrote the plays attributed to him, including leading actors such as Sir Mark Rylance and Sir Derek Jacobi. It is the longest whodunit in literary history.

*Cheyneygates where Elizabeth Woodville sought sanctuary*

A large majority of scholars still believes that Shakespeare was the author, despite some of the obvious worries, such as - how on earth could a man from a background of illiteracy have written so many plays, with such detailed knowledge of so many subjects and places here and abroad?

A curious factor is the number of the authors put forward as rival claimants who have some sort of link with Thorney Island. At school, I thought Francis Bacon, who would have been a familiar sight in Whitehall, was the true author because the obscure Latin word in Love's Labours Lost, honorificabilitudinitatibus, was claimed to be an anagram of: "Hi ludi, F. Baconis nati, tuiti orbi", translated as "These works, born of Francis Bacon are preserved for the world".

That lasted until someone used the same letters in the same anagram to prove that the real author was Ben Jonson, a local Westminster boy who was educated at Westminster School and is buried, standing up, in the Abbey.

Other candidates include Sir Henry Neville who lived in Tothill Street which led to the western entrance to Thorney, and was an active member of Parliament across the road, and William Stanley, 6th Earl of Derby, a member of the Privy Council and patron of Derby's Men who performed at court. Christopher Marlowe, another candidate, would have been familiar with Whitehall whether due to his activities as a spy or as a playwright. Mary Herbert, Countess of Pembroke, one of the few female contenders for the authors, had connections to Westminster through her position as a prominent noblewoman and literary patron in Elizabethan and Jacobean England. Even Queen Elizabeth I has been mentioned as a candidate, as has Amelia Lanier (mentioned elsewhere) and Sir Walter Raleigh who was executed in Old Palace Yard and buried in St Margaret's Church.

Edward de Vere, the 17th Earl of Oxford, the current favourite, was a frequent presence in Whitehall as Lord Chamberlain and was married in the Royal Palace. The list could go on. None of them has a proven claim to the authorship, but is it too much to speculate that the authorship question might have been a source of gossip among themselves? Shakespeare is almost certainly the true author and even if he isn't, it is likely to have been someone else with a Thorney Island link.

Shakespeare is not buried in Westminster Abbey, although he has a memorial there, installed well over 100 years after his death. His remains are in his local church Holy Trinity in Stratford upon Avon despite efforts from time to time to have him moved to what is regarded by some as his spiritual home in the Abbey.

This has given rise to suggestions that Shakespeare has a kind of ethereal presence in the Abbey, not because he is buried there but because he isn't. Poets' Corner is known around the globe for celebrating all that is memorable about our poets and playwrights except for one: the greatest of them all: William Shakespeare.

However, visitors could be passing actual mementos of Shakespeare without realising it. When Edmund Spenser was buried in Poets Corner, according to the contemporary historian William Camden, his hearse was attended by poets and "mournfull Elegies and Poems with the Pens that wrote them thrown into his Tomb". It is a reasonable assumption that Shakespeare could have been among these poets in which case the pen that Shakespeare used and possibly an elegy written in his own hand could still be lying in Spenser's tomb.

But, wait. In 1938, the Francis Bacon Society got permission to open up Edmund Spenser's grave to solve this problem once and for all but there was a new problem: they got the wrong tomb. The mystery rolls on.

# 19: The tragic tale of a little known King of England, Harold Harefoot

*Harold Harefoot with the pet hare which gave him his nickname*

Harold Harefoot is one of the saddest stories of Thorney Island. He is hardly known at all, even under his official title of King Harold. He was one of the two feuding sons of King Cnut (or Canute) and he ruled England for five years after Canute's death until 1040, including several as Regent. He died in his early 20s and was buried in St Peter's Abbey, a precursor to Westminster Abbey.

But not for long. After Harefoot's death, his half brother, Harthacnut, still seething with rage that he should have been King and not Harefoot, arrived from Denmark with a fleet of 60 ships to re-enforce his claim to the throne.

After being crowned, he had Harold's body exhumed only a few months after his death, then beheaded, and thrown into the River Thames or into a fen nearby. Subsequently, according to contemporary accounts, the body was retrieved from the river by a fisherman and reburied at St. Clement Danes Church in the Strand, which was a destination for Danes in London. The spot where he was buried in St Clements, if indeed he was, has not yet been found. What it clearly needs is for a team like the one that found Richard III's corpse under a carpark in Leicester to get cracking.

We don't know much about what Harefoot did during his reign, partly because he was ill much of the time and partly because the history of the period was initially written by the "winners" from the Harthacnut camp. It is maybe for this reason that some historians have speculated not on what he did but on what might have happened if he had not died so quickly in his early 20s.

*The death throes of Harthacnut*

The argument goes something like this:

Had Harold lived and kept hold of his throne then Harthacnut might never have returned to England in which case Edward the Confessor would never have returned from Normandy. If there had been no King Edward it would probably have meant no Norman conquest and no William the Conqueror. Sometimes the "ifs" of history are more interesting than the actuality.

Fate didn't smile too kindly on Harthacnut either. He collapsed and died at a wedding celebration for his friend Tovi the Proud, a rich Danish official, across the river from Thorney Island in Lambeth. He died, aged only 24, from an excess bout of alcohol, or a heart attack, or both. Be warned.

# 20: Meet the French governor of Duck Island in St James's Park

*Duck Island, St James's Park*

One of the curious inhabitants of Poets' Corner in Westminster Abbey - established to laud the achievements of English poetry - is a French nobleman Charles de Martguetel de Saint-Denis, seigneur de Saint-Évremond. He apparently spoke little or no English and, according to the critic Irving Lowens, he wrote "sparkling French prose and facile French verse". He was also a skeptic who refused the last rltes.

Saint-Évremond was buried - against his desire for a modest funeral - in Westminster Abbey a few yards from the memorial to Shakespeare who was interred in his local church, Holy Trinity in Stratford-upon-Avon. How come Saint-Évremond managed to be buried in the Abbey?

It is, of course, not what you know, but who you know. Saint-Évremond became a buddy of Charles II, not least because he introduced Charles to French champagne which he became very fond of. One should add that this was not champagne as we know it today, because it had no bubbles. French wine bottles in those days were too fragile, and would burst if there was a secondary fermentation, whereas Britain, using coal-fired kilns rather than wood-fired ones was able to make much stronger bottles, which is how the English came to invent the "methode champenoise" at least 20 years before the French.

Historians are not agreed on whether Charles II was a good French speaker, but he must have been proficient as his mother was French and he spent nine years of his exile in France. Saint-Évremond had fled from France in disgrace in the early 1660s, after incurring the wrath of Cardinal Mazarin during the reign of Louis IV. He soon became a social success among aristocrats in London.

Charles II did an extraordinary thing. He made Saint-Évremond Governor of Duck Island in St James Park where ducks were lured into captivity using decoys before being served at the King's table. Duck Island was, and still is, tiny. The governorship for which he was paid £300 guineas a year, a lot of money in those days, must have been the smallest and most easily governable territory in Britain, if not the world.

St Évremond's tomb. Shakespeare's memorial is on the other side of the wall

Évremond wasn't the only governor of Duck Island. In 1773 Queen Caroline revived the post by giving it to Stephen Duck, an agricultural labourer known as the "Thresher Poet" a kind of Rabbie Burns of the West Country. Who says monarchs don't have a sense of humour? Sadly, Duck of Duck Island did not achieve the lasting fame of Burns, nor was he buried in Westminster Abbey.

Évremond's name is enjoying a mini revival. The French champagne house Tattinger co-purchased a large acreage of prime agricultural land in Kent to take advantage of how global warming has boosted the UK's ability to make good wines, particularly sparkling. The new wine is to be called Domain Evremond. What Charles de St. Denis, Seigneur de Saint Evremond, would have said about a Champagne that was sparkling and not still, as he knew it, can only be guessed at.

# 21: The tallest tomb in the Abbey

This is the memorial and grave of Henry Carey, the first Baron Hunsdon (1526-1596) and his extended family. It is the tallest of many tall monuments in the Abbey reaching 36 feet, made of alabaster and marble with an all-embracing motto (in French) "As I find it."

Hunsdon himself, it is fair to point out, wasn't what you might expect. He was the illegitimate son of Mary Boleyn (sister of Anne Boleyn) and some say of Henry VIII himself. Hunsdon proved himself a brave soldier and was festooned with well paid jobs. From 1594 until his death in 1596 he was patron of the Lord Chamberlain's Men, the company for which Shakespeare wrote many of his plays and which became the King's Men under James I: but whenever I look at this tomb I am thinking of someone else.

The inscription on Hunsdon's monument refers to "his dearest wife" Anne with whom he had 10 or possibly 13 children. There is no reference, unsurprisingly, to his dearest mistress, Amelia Lanier, who is of some interest in her own right. She was Hunsdon's mistress for at least for ten years from 1587 when she was 18 years old.

It ended when she became pregnant and was married off by Hunsdon to a cousin of hers, Alphonse Lanier, with a generous settlement (though the affair apparently continued). He was over 40 years older than her but it appears to have been a happy relationship. She lived partly at Hunsdon's palace, Somerset House, between the Strand and the Thames and partly in Longditch (today's Storey's Gate) on the edge of Thorney Island.

Amelia was thought for a while by some experts to

have been the dark lady of Shakespeare's sonnet 130 and by others, such as John Hudson, author of "Shakespeare's Dark Lady" to have been the actual author of Shakespeare's works. (Details in Chapter 22)

# 22: The Lord, the tomb and the mistress

Storey's Gate – named after Edward Storey, Charles II's bird keeper – runs from Tothill Street by Parliament Square to St James's Park. It used to be called Longditch because it ran alongside a stretch of water, which wound its way from Tothill Street to today's Whitehall where it flowed under a bridge into the Thames. It is also the scene of one of the world's ongoing literary mysteries. Here lived Amelia Lanier (1569-1645), thought by some to have been the "Dark Lady" of Shakespeare's sonnets and, by some, even to have been the actual author of his works.

Lanier – whose forename is sometimes spelled Emelia or Aemilia, and her surname sometimes Lanyer – was born in Spitalfields of a highly musical Italian-Jewish family from near Venice, who were prominent musicians in the Tudor courts. At the age of six, she lived in the home of Susan Bertie, the Countess of Kent who, highly unusually for the times, was a protagonist for education for women. This not only hugely helped Amelier's literary development, but also eased her way into aristocratic circles which later paid dividends.

She purchased a house in Longditch with considerable help from Henry Carey, Lord Hunsdon, whose mistress she had been since she was 18 years old (he was over 40 years older than her) and whose baby she would eventually be carrying. According to the diary of Simon Forman, her astrologer whom she had consulted, she was "maintained in great pomp" with an allowance of 20 pounds a year.

Lord Hunsdon was the son of Anne Boleyn's sister Mary, who was Henry VIII's mistress before he fell for Anne. More particularly, he was the patron of the Lord Chamberlain's Men, Shakespeare's acting troupe. So, with her links to Hunsdon and her geographic closeness to Whitehall, not to mention her musical family, which participated in lots of royal plays and masques, it would be very surprising if Lanier was not at least acquainted with Shakespeare.

But Lanier doesn't any longer need an association with Shakespeare, whether literary or romantic, to ensure her place in history. She is now recognised as a formidable figure in her own right, being one of the very first women to publish a book of poetry and also a pioneer of proto-feminism 200 years before Mary Wollstonecraft. Her Salve Deus Rex Judaeorum (1611) is a Christian poem told from a feminist point of view. She even dared to suggest in her verse that it may not have been Eve who tempted Adam in the Garden of Eden, but the other way round. Glory be. She also wrote a poem, "Description of Cookham", claimed to be the first country house poem in English.

Amelia was not celebrated in her own time even though she survived until she was 76, but what she achieved would surely have surely qualified her for a burial in Poets' Corner in Westminster Abbey had burial in that space not been, and still is, a men-only monopoly. What a shame there isn't a little space on Hunsdon's memorial where a discreet effigy of Amelia could be secreted.

Did she write Shakespeare's works? Several books claim she did, including a recent one by John Hudson ("Shakespeare's Dark Lady") which argues, among numerous other things, that there is so much hidden Jewish imagery in the plays that they must have been written by a Jewish person. I was quite impressed with the evidence and would have been even more impressed had I not read another book shortly before which chronicles the amazing amount of Catholic

*Amelia Lanier and Storey's Gate*

imagery hidden in the text which purports to prove that Shakespeare was a Catholic. The Shakespeare authorship question is already the world's longest literary who-dun-it and shows no signs of flagging.

One of Shakespeare's Dark Lady sonnets includes lines which have been linked to Nicholas Hilliard's miniature of Lanier (see inset photo above):

"My mistress' eyes are nothing like the sun;

Coral is far more red, than her lips red:

If snow be white, why then her breasts are dun;

If hairs be wires, black wires grow on her head."

There is a surprising amount of information about the inhabitants of Longditch, going back to the 12th century, but sadly not enough about one of its most enigmatic inhabitants, who, had history run a different course, would surely have been buried in Poet's Corner across the road from Longditch. This who-dun-it rolls on and on...

# 23: Westminster School - the history behind the wealth and celebrities

Westminster School can give rise to different conversations. It is embarrassingly well endowed with resources at a time when the country is supposed to be aiming to be a fairer place. It is also well known as a producer of celebrated people on an industrial scale. They range from Ben Jonson and Christopher Wren back then, to recent alumni A A Milne, John Spedon Lewis, founder of the John Lewis Partnership, Helena Bonham Carter and a clutch of Nobel Prize winners, not to mention seven prime ministers in between. What is less well known is the wealth of history within its walls as it is a busy school only open to the public on a few visits a year.

Parts of the school's buildings date to the 11th century, even older than most of the current Abbey.

A good place to start is Dean's Yard, which is open to the public, from its entrance on Parliament Square near the Abbey shop. After a few yards you can turn left past College Hall, now used as a dining room by boarding pupils. It is reckoned to be one of the finest examples of a medieval refectory anywhere. It was where Elizabeth I used to come to witness Westminster pupils performing their traditional play in Latin,

It was part of Cheynegates, the Dean of Westminster's traditional residence,claimed to be the oldest surviving continuously occupied residence in London. It stretches along one side of Dean's Yard to the entrance to the Cloisters which is also the entrance to the historic Cellarium café which is open to the public. It was in Cheynegates where another queen, Elizabeth Woodville, wife of Edward IV, twice sought sanctuary most famously in 1483 with her daughters and son Richard, who with his brother, the future Edward V, became the Princes in the Tower of London.

Curiously, no one seems to agree when the school was actually started but it is likely to have been around 1179 when Pope Alexander III made it compulsory for

*College Hall where Elizabeth I witnessed Westminster pupils perform a play in Latin*

monasteries to encourage education. Since then, Henry VIII is credited with founding the school, or at least ensuring that it continued after the Reformation, but Elizabeth I is regarded by many as more important as the re-founder of the school. The aim was to educate poor children, an ambition that was re-affirmed by Elizabeth whose statutes declared that 40 scholars should be chosen based on "gentleness of disposition, ability, learning, good character and poverty". The school tries to maintain these principles, though poverty has been somewhat neglected since, at the time of writing, fees are now over £50,000 a year for boarders.

But if the school has drifted from its educational moorings, its buildings are a constant reminder of its medieval heritage.

If you continue walking along the side of Dean's Yard you will see the original

*Henry VIII's faded coat of arms above the original entrance to the school in Dean's Yard*

entrance to the school in all its faded majesty with Henry VIII's original coat of arms barely discernible above. This was where Alice Liddell, who inspired the book Alice in Wonderland was born.

This is a private part of the school, but if you manage to get on to one of the official visits you would go through the entrance and soon come across a reception room under which the remains of the 40ft square Great Kitchen of the monastery dating back to the 1060s have been preserved under thick glass.

It was built in the 15th century, but is on the site of an earlier one first constructed during the 1060s around

the time of William the Conqueror.

One nearby door led to the misericord (Latin for "act of mercy") where monks could eat meat which was forbidden by the rules of St Benedict when they were eating in the main dining hall.

Close by is Little Dean's Yard, regarded as the centre of activities for pupils between lessons. It is dominated on one side by Ashburnham House which once contained the Cotton Library, a unique collection of books which was a crucial founding donation to the British Museum (since moved to the British Library). The

*Part of the medieval kitchen*

collection was moved here from elsewhere to protect it from possible fire hazards only itself to be hit by a fire at Ashburnham in 1721 which destroyed some of its priceless treasures. This is described in more detail in chapter XX but it is worth pointing out that it was called Ash-burn-ham long before the accident.

The real gem of Ashburnham is in its garden, a step back in time where you can see remains of the actual medieval wall of the monks' refectory at the back, partially obscured by a tree. Early meetings of MPs in the embryonic Parliament were shunted from place to place, depending on what was available, including the Painted Chamber and the Chapter House, but the refectory became the regular place for meetings of the Commons for many years until MPs moved into St Stephen's Chapel in the 16th century. The tiny protrusion on the left of the photo is part of the roof of the school's Eton Fives court where the curious game of Eton Fives is still played.

What happened to the other Refectory wall on the nearside which would have occupied much of the lawn? There was a theory that it was pulled down by Protector Somerset as part of his pillaging campaign to provide stone for his Somerset House in the Strand, as

a few years later he tried to pull down Saint Margaret's church for the same reason, but was repulsed. It turns out that the Abbey itself dismantled the wall but left the other one standing as it was part of the cloister on the other side.

The biggest feature of the school is the main hall, originally built in the 1090s as a dormitory for the monks and now used for assemblies, plays and prayers. Kim Philby, the spy, once took part in a play in the hall. Pupils were taught here from 1599 with the upper and lower schools separated by a curtain hung from a 16th century pig iron bar which Wikipedia assures us "remains the largest piece of pig iron in the world". That is almost the main memory carried away from this historic room that is curiously lacking in strong visual impact partly due to the coats of arms of former pupils spreadeagled around the walls.

This is a fitting place to say Goodbye to a spectacularly successful academic school, replete with history which perhaps has yet to come to terms with a slowly changing society. It is almost grotesquely endowed with facilities compared with neighbouring state schools.

*The garden with the Eton Fives court on the left*

*The school hall dating back to 1090*

# 24: The huge fortune behind this tomb at St Margaret's church

St Margaret's Church yard in Parliament Square is not short of famous dead bodies. It is the resting place of William Caxton, Sir Walter Raleigh, Wenceslaus Hollar, the brilliant engraver of London, and the largest number of regicides (of Charles I) you'll find anywhere.

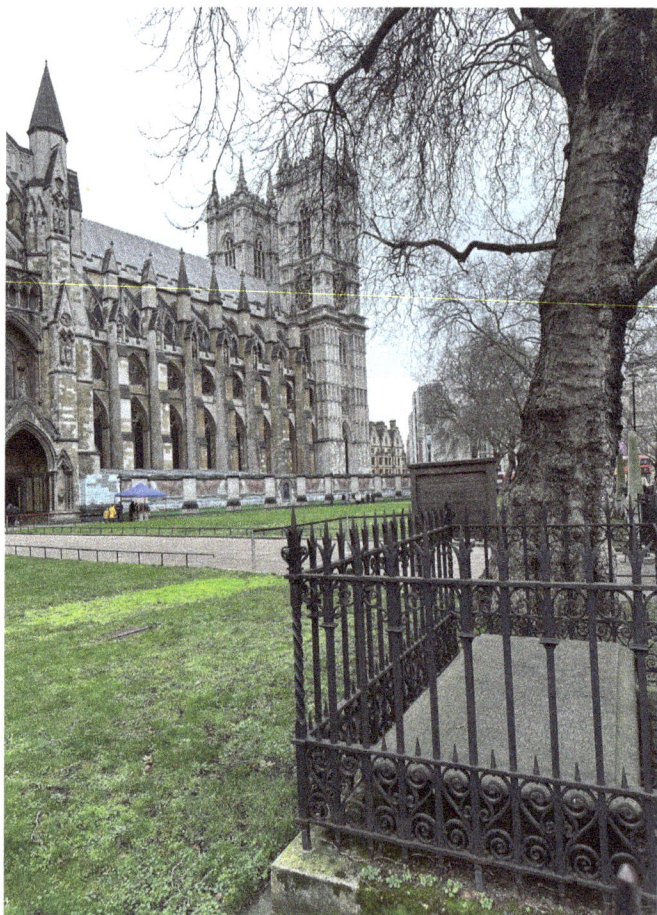

*The Davis tomb in St Margaret's Churchyard with Westminster Abbey behind*

But of all the hundreds of people buried in the precinct, curiously, there is only one tomb that is above ground. It is near the road obscured by a plane tree and usually completely ignored by passers-by. It is the source of the greatest property wealth this country has ever known, which helped to influence the shape of London. Here lies Alexander Davis, (or Davies) father of Mary Davis - who is also buried here (as Mary Tregonwell). He was a scrivener, who died of the plague, heavily in debt, in July 1665 but owning quite a bit of land. Mary, who was only seven months old when he died, eventually inherited 500 acres of what was then regarded as almost worthless pasture, meadow and swamp land, but which we know today as Belgravia, Pimlico and Mayfair. It also included land along Millbank where Peterborugh House (below) was constructed which eventually became the London mansion of the Grosvenors until they moved into Grosvenor Square.

If you adjust for inflation and value Mary's inheritance (which is still in the Grosvenor family) at today's values it would have laid the ground for Thorney Island's first billionaire and quite possibly the first potential female billionaire anywhere.

To cut a long and complicated story short, Mary, having apparently been betrothed to someone else earlier aged 7, was married aged 12 to a little known baronet in the north, Sir Thomas Grosvenor, who at the time was busy building his family seat, Eaton Hall. By all accounts they had a happy 20 years together despite Mary becoming mentally ill. Sir Thomas died in 1700 which left Mary as the sole heir of what became

*The Grosvenors' London pad along Millbank*

Britain's biggest estate until, still mentally ill, she died in 1730. Somewhat ironically, the vast estate bequeathed by a woman was then passed on down the Grosvenor line through a succession of eldest sons. It was ever thus.

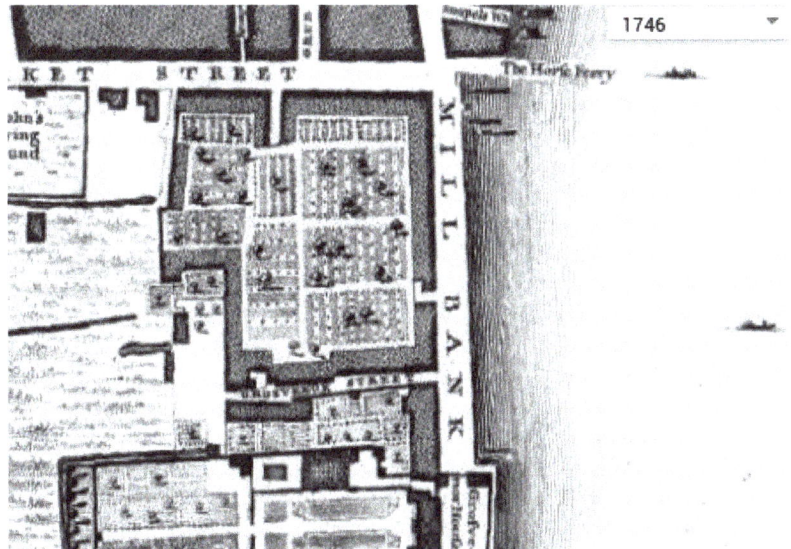

*The Grosvenor's estate at Millbank*

# 25: Sir Peter Warren, Thorney Island's unsung billionaire MP

In 1716, a boy from Warrenstown, County Meath in Ireland joined the British navy, aged only 13 as an ordinary seaman. This was illegal as both of his parents were Catholics, which should have disbarred him from the English navy in those days - but they let that pass. By the end of a distinguished naval career, he became a very rich man owning over a thousand acres in America, including 300 acres in Greenwich Village. At today's prices he would quite likely be a Thorney Island billionaire.

Sir Peter Warren has one of the most extraordinary tombs in Westminster Abbey, with a highly unusual sculpture to commemorate him accompanied by an epitaph by Dr Johnson no less. It represents Hercules placing a bust of Sir Peter, made by the distinguished French sculptor Roubiliac, on a pedestal watched over by an erotically clad female figure representing Navigation. Roubiliac carried realism to the extreme by leaving marks from smallpox on Warren's face. The model for Hercules, believe it or not, was a bare knuckle fighter Jack Broughton who, rather surprisingly, is also buried in the Abbey. There is a plaque on the floor of the East Cloister to commemorate his achievements.

Sir Peter did not come from quite as humble a background as may have been suggested. The fact that "Warren" came from "Warrenstown" gives a clue that this wasn't a typical rags to riches story, but that takes nothing away from his extraordinary achievements. To cut a long story short, after being brought up by his Catholic parents as a Protestant in order to have a future at sea, he had a distinguished naval career ending up as Admiral of the Fleet patrolling American waters to keep the French Navy out. Among the successes of his team were the capture of 24 ships in four months in 1744 and supporting the forces of Massachusetts in capturing Louisbourg from the French after a 47 day siege in 1745. This expedition not only earned him a knighthood and promotion to rear-Admiral, but a small fortune as well.

In those days officers were allowed to keep much of the booty won and this, together with gifts and a bit of land speculation enabled Warren to acquire thousands of acres in America including 300 acres in what we today call Greenwich Village where he built a mansion for himself and his rich American wife Susannah Delancey.

A New York website completes the story: "It was in 1747 that our hero was summoned to London, to enter Parliament from 1747 to 1752 (as MP for Westminster) and from that time on was a bright particular star in English society. Known as "the richest man in England," he was a truly magnificent figure in a magnificent day. Lady Warren, who was still a beauty and a wit, was a great favourite at Court, and writers of the day declared her to be the cleverest woman in all England".

The towns of Warren, Rhode Island and Warren, New Hampshire are named after him as are streets in Charleston, South Carolina, Louisbourg and New York City. Warren Street off Tottenham Court Road, commemorates Sir Peter's wife.

Little known fact: George Bernard Shaw said that a scandal in this street inspired the name of the leading character in his play Mrs Warren's Profession.

Sacred to the Memory
of Sir PETER WARREN
Knight of the Bath,
Vice Admiral of the Red Squadron
of the British Fleet,
and Member of Parliament
for the City and Liberty of Westminster.

He derived his Descent from an antient Family of IRELAND,
his Fame and Honours from his Virtues and Abilities.
How eminently these were displayed,
with what Vigilance and Spirit they were exerted,
in the various Services wherein he had the Honour to Command,
and the Happiness to Conquer,
will be more properly recorded in the Annals of
GREAT BRITAIN.
On this Tablet, Affection with truth must say,
that deservedly esteemed in private Life,
and universally renowned for his publick Conduct,
The judicious and gallant Officer,
possed all the amiable Qualities of the Friend,
the Gentleman and the Christian.
MIGHTY

ERECTED

THE
WILLIAM
FOUR
BORN DECEM

# 26: How two medieval schools on Thorney survived until today

This is about two pioneering 17th century schools around Thorney Island which opened within ten years of each other and which are still with us today in one form or another. They are distinct from Westminster School, a public (ie private) school which still operates in the shadow of the Abbey.

In 1688, a group of local people founded a new school in Duck Lane (now called St Matthew's Street) by voluntary subscription which became known as the Blewcoat School because of the colour of the pupils' uniforms. The aim was to teach 20 local children in the deprived local parishes of St John and St Margaret to read, write and improve their religious knowledge. Twenty years later, it moved to Brewer's Green in Caxton Street, quite likely a reference to William Green (or Greene), a local brewer who financed it, where it still is today. The beautiful Grade 1 listed building, which has signs of being influenced

*The beautiful Blewcoat School from the back*

by Christopher Wren, is still standing today though it has long since ceased to be a school.

Barely ten years later on 9th January 1698, another school, Greycoat Hospital School (above) was founded in Broad Sanctuary in front of Westminster Abbey in the heart of Thorney Island. Being within the Sanctuary meant that it was close to the home of criminals who were able to claim freedom from the long arm of the law. James I abolished the Sanctuary in 1624, but the culture of criminality it engendered just moved a few roads away to the area around Old Pye Street. This was the centre of what Charles Dickens later popularised as the "Devils' Acre" which was close to Greycoat School.

Like the Blewcoat School, Greycoats was funded by eight local parishioners, to teach the poor of the parish to become workers, good citizens and solid Christians. Initially it was just for boys, but in 1701 the governors purchased an old workhouse in Tothill Fields to found a school for boys and girls called Greycoat Hospital. It is still there today, now a top rated all-girls Comprehensive school, on the same site though in a more modern building. Part of its heritage still survives to remind everyone of its history.

*Greycoat Hospital School*

Every day pupils walk over the original medieval flagstones of the workhouse.

In the case of the Blewcoat School, the pupils eventually became part of an amalgamation which led to integration with others to become today's Westminster City School, but their actual original building is still there in all its glory in Caxton Street, a gem among the suffocating tower blocks around it, the only late 17th century building in that part of Westminster.

These schools were pioneering. They were not the first of their kind because a similar free school had been founded in 1512 at the Savoy, but that was by a King (Henry Vll), not by individuals. They were at the forefront of a process which centuries later would evolve into a national network of free schools.

Both Blewcoat and Greycoat schools - not to mention the Brown Coat, Green Coat, and Black Coat Schools - all sprung from the "turf wars" among religious schools in the 17th century when Catholics and Protestants vied to enlist poverty-stricken children growing up in the slums at a time when there was no state education.

An excerpt from a parchment roll from around 1700 says it all:

"In the late reign, the Roman Catholick Priests and Jesuites were busie in making Proselytes and to that end set up Free Schools in the Savoy and other places in and about the City of London inviting all poor children to be educated by them gratis…"

Anglicans responded in kind. If street kids were to be given an education for nothing then it had better be Anglican and not Roman Catholic.

It was from such philanthropic beginnings that our present system of secular and religious education took shape.

At a time when most of Westminster has been subjected to extensive rebuilding we should be grateful that the buildings of three schools dating back over many centuries are still there: Westminster (public) school, Blewcoat School and Greycoat Hospital School.

# 27: The Devil's Acre. Fagin's den and the deepest depths of depravity

Thorney Island undoubtedly had its own problems, host as it was to criminals who could claim Sanctuary to avoid arrest, but it was also home to rich people associated with Parliament, the law courts, the Abbey and for hundreds of years, the royal palace. This should not blind us to the utterly horrific conditions endured by residents barely a hundred yards away. It was almost certainly the biggest contrast of riches to poverty anywhere in London or indeed the whole country.

When Charles Dickens called the streets around Old Pye Street (pictured below after improvements) "The Devil's Acre" he knew what he was talking about. He had been a parliamentary reporter nearby and was involved with philanthropists trying to improve conditions. Several other parts of London could claim to be as destitute – Shoreditch, Saint Giles and Turnmill Street for a start – but none had the abominable combination of destitution and criminality that have darkened this ghetto.

In the first edition of his Household Words (1850), Dickens described the neighbourhood as "begirt by scenes of indescribable infamy and pollution; the blackest tide of moral turpitude that flows in the capital rolls its filthy wavelets up to the very walls of Westminster Abbey."

J E Smith, vestry clerk of the parish of St Margaret and St John the Evangelist, gave another grim insight: "During the cholera epidemic of 1848, a medical gentleman was called to visit a sufferer in one of the streets on which the church now abuts. While stooping over the poor creature to administer medicine, with which he was provided in readiness, his coat pockets were emptied of the contents by the dying woman's husband!" Later during the first services in the new church, completed in 1851, the inhabitants of the notorious alleyways nearby interrupted the worship by beating empty barrels.

Old Pye Street in the late 19th century

Thomas Beames in his "The Rookeries of London" (1852) wrote that New Court in the Devil's Acre (probably off Old Pye Street) contained twelve houses, with six rooms in each: "I have seen and known as many as seventy- two persons living in one of these houses; and I recollect, in the course of three months, sixty-nine young persons being transported, and one executed at Newgate, out of No 2". He added: "I might go on describing the streets and courts of the district; but, after all I should write, it would give a faint idea of what I have witnessed. I have seen upwards of forty policemen beat out of Old Pye Street, by the inhabitants, while attempting to take a thief".

Does 72 people in one house sound unbelievably high? The 1861 census for Old Pye Street showed a single lodging in this street was home to over 120 people. Such unbelievably chronic overcrowding was partly the result of the construction of Victoria Street which was opened in 1851. New apartments were built, but those not lucky enough to gain a flat in the new Peabody estates - which required applicants to have a wage-earning job - were left with nowhere to live. Most went across the river to Lambeth but many remained to add to the chronic overcrowding of the area around Old Pye Street worsened by outbreaks of cholera.

This is how the Revd Richard Malone, Vicar of the local church St Matthew's, described his parish in 1901, well after the construction of Victoria Street was supposed to have improved the area: "The state of the streets was appalling; groups of gamblers were scattered at every corner and the police dared not interfere."

He adds of a nearby street: "Many of the houses have no flooring in their passages and there is nothing for the barefooted children to stand upon at the black damp uneven earth. A child, dirty and nearly naked, was hanging out the one of the old-fashioned casement windows and in the summer time it is no unusual thing to see about 50 course women exhibiting themselves in the same manner". He added: "Of all the criminal districts in London it is now the worst."

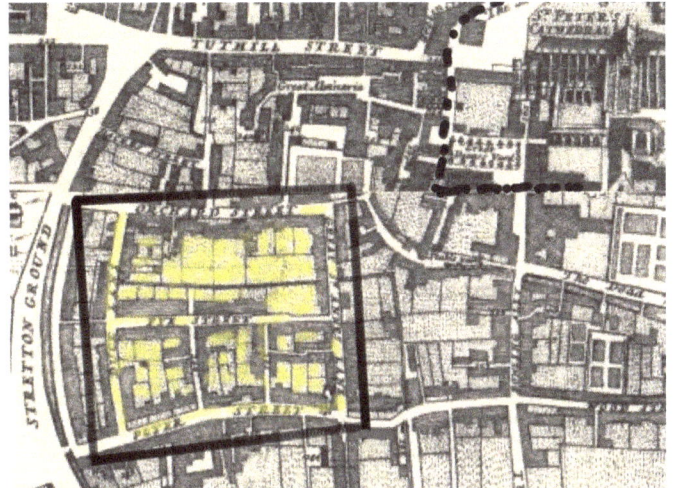

*The "Devil's Acre" (shaded yellow) very close to the Abbey precinct (dotted line)*

Old Pye Street where the restored houses in the painting (above) look like desirable residences for a family of four was the bleeding heart of the Devil's Acre.

This painting was done some time after the "improvements" when the new Victoria Street bulldozed its way through the slums, but the size of each building would have been the same.

John Hollingshead, who had worked with Dickens on Household Words, walked down Old Pye Street to St Ann's Lane which in happier times had been the home of Henry Purcell and wrote: "Enter, a narrow street called St Anne's Lane, glance at a fearful side place called St Ann's Court, and wonder if ever such filth and squalor can be exceeded. The court had every feature of a sewer, and a long puddle of filth soaked in a hollow centre". He described Old Pye Street as an "openly acknowledged high street of thieves and prosti-tutes" and added: "It has no mock modesty about it, no desire to conceal its real character. Threepenny "homes for travellers" abound on both sides-yellow, sickly, unwholesome places, many of them far below the level of the road, and entered by a kind of pit. Many of the houses have no flooring on their passages; and there is nothing for the barefooted children to stand upon but the black, damp, uneven earth".

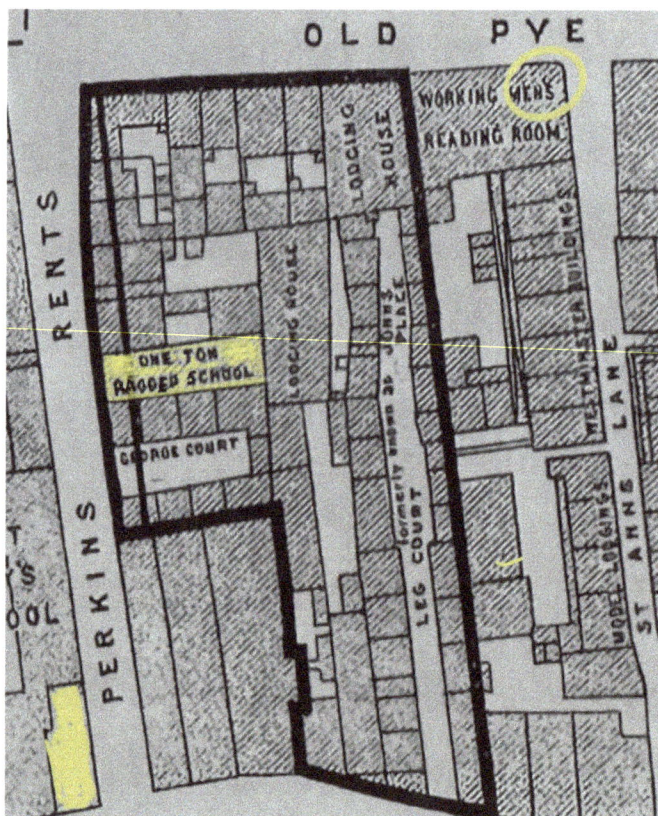

*Today's Speaker pub is marked by a yellow oblong bottom left. Above is the Ragged School of pickpockets before it moved to Old Pye Street (circled). Source unknown*

Further along Old Pye Street in a road called Perkin's Rents was a pub called The One Tun (map above and photo below). It was, in effect, a School of Fobology (pickpocketing), almost certainly the inspiration for Fagin's Den in Oliver Twist even though the fictional version was diplomatically located elsewhere (Jacob's Island). The photo was taken in 1870 when the pub had been converted into a ragged school by Adeline Cooper, a wealthy philanthropist, backed by Lord Shaftesbury, who was shocked by the conditions in the Devil's Acre, particularly the plight of street children. It provides a rare photographic example of what the street looked like in earlier times. .

*The One Tun*

It is difficult for us to imagine the scale of depravity. This was at a time when Britain was boasting about its material success to the rest of the world, which we nowadays realise was frequently based on the slave trade. Under Prince Albert's guidance, the Great Exhibition of 1851 in Hyde Park was not only a showpiece for Britain's industrial prowess but - unlike similar exhibitions around the world - it invited other countries to compete

*One of Prince Albert's model dwellings for the poor now at Kensington Park*

- so confident were we of our superiority. This example of Britain at its best in Hyde Park was happening only a few miles from Britain at its worst - The Devil's Acre.

To his credit, Prince Albert wanted to include in the exhibition some model dwellings for poorer people but he was overruled by his own board. It wasn't the sort of thing they wanted to draw attention to. Prince Albert's model dwellings were constructed near the Great Exhibition, but not in it and were later pulled down and transferred to Kennington Park where they can still be seen, a forerunner to the Peabody buildings.

How could the men of God (no women apart from Queen Victoria) and the rulers of a vast empire have let this social and moral apartheid happen? We have to go back to Edward the Confessor who reigned from 1042 until 1066. He founded the Abbey and turned the precincts into a sanctuary to which criminals could go and be free from the hand of the law. This was so well observed that not even kings would dare to disregard it under pain of excommunication. James I abolished the rights of sanctuary in the early 1600s, but the culture of criminality had taken root and helps to explain why what became the Devil's Acre continued to attract criminals for centuries afterwards.

# 28: How the horse trough rescued London

**METROPOLITAN**
## Drinking Fountain & Cattle Trough
### ASSOCIATION.
*Supported entirely by Voluntary Contributions.*

Offices: VICTORIA HOUSE, 111, VICTORIA ST., WESTMINSTER, S.W

*President*—His Grace the DUKE OF WESTMINSTER, K.G., &c., &c.
*Chairman of Committee and Treasurer*—JOSEPH FLY, Esq.
*Secretary*—M. W. MILTON.

This is the ONLY AGENCY for providing
**FREE SUPPLIES OF WATER FOR MAN AND BEAST**
in the STREETS of LONDON,

He co-founded and chaired the Metropolitan Drinking Fountain and Cattle Trough Association (MDFCTA) in 1859 with its HQ near Parliament in Victoria Street with his co-founder Edward Thomas Wakefield. It provided free, clean drinking water for the public and troughs for the animals including an estimated 100,000 horses in London. Horses were the main means of transport and they needed water to survive the day. By 1900, the number of working horses in London had soared to an astonishing 300,000. Without water troughs. London might have ground to a halt. By this time there were about 800 horse troughs in London, mainly due to the voluntary initiative of the MDFCTA.

There are reckoned to be over 100 original troughs still in London often repurposed as micro-gardens or works of art and all of them reminders of the 19th century city.

The first drinking fountain was erected in 1859 on the boundary wall of the church of St Sepulchre-without-

Thorney Island has produced a number of distinguished MPs, but none quite like Samuel Gurney. He was an independent member for Penryn and Falmouth for eleven years from 1857 to 1868. Despite holding office for over a decade, he never actually spoke in Parliament during a debate, not even a recorded aside. Gurney (1816–1882) was a banker and a philanthropist, as well as a politician. He doesn't sound like a model MP, but it could be argued that he was what MPs ought to be like. Instead of taking part in the Westminster talking shop, he actually went out and did things with voluntary help, which in an ideal world would have been voted through by Parliament at public expense.

*A surviving horse trough in Smithfield in front of St Bartholomew's hospital*

Newgate on Snow Hill, where it can still be observed today (see photo below). It soon became very popular, serving around 7,000 people a day.

In 1867, the association started to include water troughs for animals, mainly horses, used for public and private transportation and commercial deliveries.

This created a new problem of disposing of the thousands of tons of horse manure left on the roads. A tongue-in-cheek article in The Times in 1894 predicted that in 50 years "every street in London will be buried under nine feet of manure". The problem wasn't finally solved until the coming of mechanised cars and lorries in the late nineteenth and early twentieth centuries.

Meanwhile, Gurney's other pioneering activities included being the first chair of the London and Provincial District Telegraph Company in 1859 which provided low cost telegrams for the general public within a 4 mile radius of Charing Cross later extended to 20 miles. It operated dozens of "stations", equivalent to today's post offices which were claimed to be no more than five minutes walk from each other.

London's first drinking fountain at St Sepulchre-without-Newgate

He was also president of the National Association for the Relief of British Miners which helped support miners when they lost income from being on strike or other hardships, another example of what has been described as his "extra-parliamentary social welfare causes". The Association carried on until it ran out of steam in 1868 and was swallowed up by the Post Office. However, Gurney is still remembered today by all the horse troughs in London and elsewhere. Not many MPs could claim such granite-solid memories, especially if they didn't speak in Parliament at all.

# 29: The secret garden that hosted Parliament

*The garden of Ashburnham House with the medieval refectory wall behind*

The garden of Ashburnham House in Little Dean's Yard, now part of Westminster School, contains a priceless piece of history. At the back is one wall of the medieval refectory where the monks ate their meals and where the embryonic House of Commons met for many years. The lower section of the wall dates back to the time of Edward the Confessor and the upper part to Edward III.

Ashburnham House is also remembered for something completely different. On 2nd October 1731, a fire broke out beneath the library in the house. It contained the priceless Cotton collection of books including the Lindisfarne Gospels, two copies of the original Magna Carta, Sir Gavin and the Green Knight and so on. As the flames found their way up the wooden panels, the billowing smoke created its own alarm. Among

*Westminster pupils in front of Ashburnham House*

the people who rushed to the rescue was an alert librarian, who threw a book out of the window in an attempt to save it. It was no ordinary book. It was the only copy in the world of one of the classics of early English literature, Beowulf. The actual manuscript was written around 1000 AD, but the poem itself is probably much older dating back to as early as 650 AD.

Contemporary records report that Dr Richard Bentley, who was looking after the Royal Collection, also housed at Ashburnham, leaped from a window holding under one arm the priceless Codex Alexandrinus, a 5th-century Greek manuscript containing most of the Old and New Testaments.

Whether he was the same person who saved Beowulf is not clear but together they helped to save the majority of the books and manuscripts - all collected by the indefatigable Sir Robert Cotton (1571–1631) - which later formed the heart of the collections of the British Library.

Thirteen manuscripts were lost and over 200 others suffered severe destruction and water damage. One of the worst losses was a unique manuscript of the Life of King Alfred the Great.

It is one of the minor ironies of history that the Cotton collection had been moved to the inappropriately named Ash-burn-ham House for safekeeping.

There had been a building on the site of Ashburnham House since the 11th century. It took its name from Charles Ashburnham, a Royalist friend of Charles II

*Ashburnham house today*

who leased it after the Restoration. It became part of Westminster School in 1882 when the Dean and Chapter bought back the property from the Crown, following an acrimonious parliamentary battle over its ownership.

Ashburnham House was the London seat of the family, which became the Earls of Ashburnham. It incorporates remains of the medieval Prior's House and its garden is the site of the monks' refectory (photo, above) where some of the earliest sittings of the House of Commons took place.

The current building incorporates the remains of the medieval Prior's House, and its garden is the site of the former monks' refectory and some of the earliest sittings of the House of Commons including when they met there to impeach Piers Gaveston during the reign of Edward ll.

The other wall of the refectory would have occupied part of the lawn of the garden. It is still a bit of a puzzle why it was pulled down. One unsubstantiated theory is that it was demolished by Protector Somerset to provide material for his proposed palace, Somerset House, on the Strand.

Footnote - the glimpse of a roof on the left side of the photograph of the garden is part of an Eton Fives Court. Although the rules were not formalised until the 18th century, its roots can be traced back to medieval times when peasants played handball against chapel walls.

# 30: The Chapter House; a building "beyond compare"

The Chapter House of Westminster Abbey has a good claim to be one of the most important small buildings in the country. It is best seen from Old Palace Yard in its full glory when the trees in front have shed their leaves in winter. It is interesting enough in its own peerless shape before looking at its history. It was built by Henry III in the mid 1250s as part of his vision to reconstruct the Abbey. It was a place where the monks could meet every day to read a "chapter" from the rule of St Benedict before discussing what was to happen during the rest of the day. It was octagonal in shape replacing an earlier round chapter house constructed by Edward the Confessor in 1050. It has been described by Sir Giles Gilbert Scott as "a structure perfect in itself". The medieval monk, Mathew Paris, referred to it as "a chapter house beyond compare".

The pathway (below) once led to a stall run by William Caxton as an adjunct to his printing press situated in the Almonry on the other side of the Abbey.

To see inside the Chapter House, however, you have to buy the standard ticket to visit the whole Abbey which is £30 at the time of writing. Until a few years ago it was free to visit the Chapter House, the Cloisters and the historic garden, but it was stopped when it was discovered that internet users were explaining how you could get into the Abbey itself from the Cloisters without paying anything.

part of Victorian "improvements". It still contains some lovely wall paintings and what is claimed to be one of the finest medieval tile pavements in England.

*Inside the Chapter House*

*Britain's oldest door*

Once inside, at the entrance to the Chapter House you pass on your right, what is confidently claimed to be the oldest door in Britain. Dendrochronology has dated the growth of the wood to between 924 and 1030 AD so it was well over 30 years before William the Conqueror's arrival in 1066. It is made from five oak planks with recessed battens and is the only surviving Anglo-Saxon door in the UK.

The sublimity of the Chapter House still shines through even though most of the wall paintings and floor tiles (dating back to the 1250s) have faded and the original stained glass windows have been replaced as

The Chapter House was the incubator of two great British institutions. The embryonic House of Commons met there in 1352 and later in the 1370s when Henry III summoned nobles and gentry from the country to this room to discuss thorny questions such as the raising of taxes, which until then had been the sole right of the King. MPs continued to meet there or in the monks' refectory until 1547 after the Reformation when Edward VI moved them across the road to St Stephen's Chapel.

*The wall paintings*

When the Commons moved out the space started to be filled with State records and documents. During the reign of James I, papers relating to the King's Bench and the Common Pleas were stored, a practice that carried on until the end of the 1850s. During this period it became a treasure trove of artefacts of English history, including the Domesday Book. These documents formed the core of the Public Records Office until it morphed into the National Archives at Kew. It is quite extraordinary for such a small room as the Chapter House to have so much history crammed into it. It remains a shame at the time of writing that the Abbey hasn't kept access to the Chapter House and the garden free of charge, but that is the way of the world.

Dean Stanley observed of the Chapter House that "almost all the struggles for liberty against the Crown must have taken place within these walls". This was a bit of an exaggeration as the Chapter House was too small to accommodate over 200 MPs on a regular basis, but it was undoubtedly a key staging post in the history of Parliament.

*The medieval pavement tiles*

*The exit to the Chapter House*

# 31: The unique Painted Chamber.
# It lasted 600 years until the 1834 fire

The Painted Chamber, which dates back to 1237, was a spectacular part of the medieval Palace of Westminster until it was destroyed by the Great Fire of 1834. It has been described as "perhaps the greatest artistic treasure lost in the fire". Actually, it may not have been completely lost as some archaeologists think that its foundations may be waiting to be unearthed - just behind the statue of Richard the Lionheart in Old Palace yard.

It was built by Henry III as the King's Chamber in a space close to St Stephen's Chapel and included a painting of the coronation of Edward the Confessor as a feature. This is not surprising as it was previously the room in which Edward the Confessor is said to have died and was intended to be the King's private apartment and a reception room to impress important visitors.

Twenty years later, Henry's eldest son, who had become Edward I, commissioned a further cycle of wall murals with religious themes. The murals were influenced by Edward's experience during the Crusades, and his hopes to return to fight in the Holy Land once again.

*The Chamber painted by William Capon when it was covered by tapestries*

However, the work was not actually commissioned until about 1292. Unlike the paintings which had been commissioned by his father, the murals painted for King Edward I, a soldier king, were all derived from stories in the Old Testament, and many of them depicted war-like images.

Over the years they were damaged by fire and riots and were eventually whitewashed and covered with tapestries. This was the state of the Painted Chamber as depicted by William Capon in the watercolour above.

The Painted Chamber hosted the so-called Good Parliament of 1376 which has been linked to the Peasants' Revolt of 1381. It attempted to expose government corruption which was all for the good, but Parliament's efforts were reversed by the highly unpopular John of Gaunt stoking public opposition. This came at a time of great hardship fanned by oppressive impositions like the hated Poll Tax, which fueled the grievances that led to the Peasants' Revolt of 1381, during which Gaunt's palace in the Strand was destroyed.

Later, the Painted Chamber was used for preparations for the trial of King Charles I. His death warrant was signed in the same room.

Thirty-six years later, the body of his son, King Charles II, would lie in state in the Painted Chamber the night before his burial in Westminster Abbey.

The Chamber, like most of the rest of the buildings, was destroyed in the horrific fire of 1834, even though parts of its thick medieval walls survived.

*The north part of the Painted Chamber by J T Smith*

It was refurbished and used by the House of Lords before being finally demolished in 1851. The Painted Chamber had survived largely intact for over 600 years. Let's hope that archaeologists who believe that its foundations still survive near the statue of Richard the Lionheart are correct.

# 32: How a monastery masterminded the biggest heist in British history

If asked in a pub quiz to name the biggest heist in British history most people would probably opt for the Great Train Robbery of 8th August 1963. Great Train Robbery? Forget it.

In the last week of April 1303, over 650 years before, was when surely the greatest robbery in British history took place. The theft of the King's Jewels and other treasures which had been stored in the crypt under the Chapter House and the neighbouring Pyx Chapel of Westminster Abbey. Their thick stone walls and fortified oak doors were thought to have been impregnable, the most secure rooms in the country.

There, gold and silver were measured in little round containers called pyxes. It had two heavy oak doors, one behind the other, each with three locks, meaning six keys were required to gain admittance.

The heist had been planned for a year. This gave the perpetrators time to do some serious preparation including the planting of some fast growing hemp seed in the Palace grounds to provide a literal cover-up as they planned their crime to burrow into the crypt. How much was stolen? The booty was estimated at £100,000 in the currency of the day - worth tens of millions of pounds in today's money. The vaulted undercroft - where the treasure was stored - still exists today and can be viewed by anyone buying a ticket (£30 at the time of writing) to visit the Abbey. It dates from about 1070 and is the oldest fabric, still standing, at Westminster.

Everything about the storage seemed secure until the arrival of Richard of Pudlicott or Pudlicote, also known as Richard de Podelicote. He was a "gentleman" wool

*An engraving apparently depicting Podnecott at work during the robbery*

*The Pyx Chamber, the oldest fabric in Westminster Abbey*

merchant from Oxfordshire who appeared to have had a grudge against King Edward I (known as Ironside or "Hammer of the Scots"), dating back to when he had been imprisoned in Flanders as a guarantor for the monarch's spiraling debts.

He had been watching the comings and goings in the Abbey, and when King Edward left to fight William Wallace (of Braveheart fame) in West Lothian, Scotland, his chance had come. Richard planned to sneak into the building. Having found a ladder nearby, he used it to gain entry to part of the Abbey where he stole a number of silver treasures which he sold and which whetted his appetite for something bigger.

So, after months of preparation and tunneling, shielded

by the hemp hedge he had planted, he waited until it was dark on 24th April and he entered the treasury for the first time. He remained inside rearranging the goods he wished to steal the next day on the 25th. With the connivance of a surprising number of monks oblivious of the Eighth Commandment ('Thou shalt not steal"), he carried out his plan.

A day later, he made off with all the bounty he wished to keep, burying much of it temporarily beneath a

*Edward I "Longshanks"*

cemetery gate behind nearby St Margaret's church.

The robbery was obviously an inside job, so Edward did what a king has to do. He arrested the Abbot of the Abbey and its 48 monks and associated servants, as they were the ones with access to the Pyx chamber. All were imprisoned in the Tower of London. The architectural historian Jeremy Ashbee says that when the loot started showing up in brothels and pawn shops. Pudlicote was arrested with £2,200 worth of stolen goods in his possession, an enormous amount in those days. He was sentenced to death in November 1305, having been carted from the Tower of London in a wheelbarrow, and hanged in the precincts of the Abbey on the Abbot's Gallows in Tothill (or Tuttle), Lane which appears to have run from Tothill Street towards the swampy ground of Tothill Fields.

Pudlicott was undoubtedly the main perpetrator and was executed. He had tried to pretend he acted alone to protect the monks, but to no avail. Alongside him, a dozen or so others were also hanged including the sub Prior and sacrist of the Abbey, but not, curiously, one of the leading suspects, William Palmer, who was known as William of the Palace because of his connections there. He sheltered some of the suspects in the Palace and, can you believe it, was also deputy keeper of the Fleet Prison. Most of the accused managed to escape execution, partly because the King did not want to fracture relations with the Abbey too much. For an exhaustive account of this unique event see Paul Doherty's book The Great Crown Jewels Robbery of 1303.

Afterwards, the royal treasures were removed to the Tower of London, but only until the undercrofts at the Abbey had been reinforced. They were then brought back to their historic resting place. Maybe the thinking was that, despite everything that had happened at the Abbey, God would still be their best guardian. And lightning wouldn't strike twice.

# 33: How shabby Canon Row turned from architecture to art and haute cuisine

*The strange beginnings of the Royal Architectural Museum (V&A)*

What did materialise in Canon Row on the first floor of the shabby building in the photograph (above) was Britain's first Architectural Museum which, after several moves, later expanded first into a College of Art and later into a technical college and then into a renowned catering college on Vincent Square. The technical college and its catering offshoot were helped by donations from the philanthropist Baroness Burdett-Coutts and by the active involvement of the great French chef Auguste Escoffier and the famed hotelier Cesar Ritz. Both were deeply concerned about the lack of skilled youngsters opting for a career in hospitality (Sounds familiar?).

The tiny alley known as Canon Row by Westminster Bridge is mainly remembered for being the site of Canon Row police station but it also marks the little known birth of a number of fascinating institutions. It may be pushing it a bit too far to claim that Canon Row was the parent of British Gas, but it was the site for the short-lived first works of The Gas Light and Coke Company, the world's first public gas company, which eventually became British Gas. The Canon Street project was soon abandoned as too small and the company moved to its new headquarters in nearby Great Peter Street. However, its origins were not forgotten. In 1960, there was a proposal to put a plaque on Canon Row police station to mark the origin of the gas company, but it did not materialise.

*Canon Row today*

Their foresight led to the establishment of today's prestigious Westminster Kingsway Catering College still in Vincent Square where Jamie Oliver and countless others learned their trade and where there is a highly regarded Escoffier restaurant run by final year students in addition to a brasserie run by other students.

It all started with the architectural museum which took off in 1851, the year of the Great Exhibition in Hyde Park, when the dream of some of Britain's most celebrated architects and artists - including George Gilbert Scott, Sir Charles Barry and John Ruskin - came true. Britain was to have its own architectural museum which opened a year later in Canon Row and was soon called The Royal Architectural Museum, thanks to backing from Queen Victoria and Prince Albert. It was totally unlike Prince Albert's world-beating extravaganza in Hyde Park. It began life on the upper floor of a dingy building used for stabling in Canon Row, a cul-de-sac. It was not destined to win any architectural prizes.

Canon Row, on the edge of Thorney Island, had seen better days. It is so named because in medieval times it was used to house the Dean and canons from St Stephen's Chapel nearby, each of which had a large garden stretching down to the Thames. On some maps it is called Channel Row because it led down to the Thames, but that was not its real name.

In the late 16th century it went through its aristocratic phase. It had been the home of the statesman William Cecil when he worked for Protector Somerset during Edward VI's reign. He left in 1561 when he purchased what became the palatial Cecil House on the Strand where the Strand Palace hotel now stands. During its

THE ARCHITECTURAL MUSEUM, WESTMINSTER.

*The interior of the architectural museum in Cannon Row*

aristocratic phase, the residents of Canon Row read like a roll call from Debrett's. They included the Earl of Derby (at Derby House), the Earl of Hertford (at Hertford House), the Earl of Lincoln (at Lincoln House) and the Earl of Sussex (at Sussex House).

Towards the end of the 18th century, Canon Row was the home of the black polymath Ignatius Sancho, probably because it was near the home of his mentor the Duke of Montagu at Montagu Houses. This was before Sancho moved across King Street (today's Whitehall) to Charles Street where there is a plaque commemorating the grocery shop he ran there. By the mid 19th century, Canon Row was clearly in decline as can be seen when it became the home of

*The architectural museum at 18 Tufton Street (The Builder, 1869)*

the somewhat shabby architectural museum and the original Elementary Drawing School.

Despite these insalubrious beginnings, within two years the museum had acquired over 6,000 objects, both casts (reproductions) and 250 original works. It clearly needed more room. Among the most valuable additions were 43 casts from Ruskin's visit to Venice.

When a government grant was removed in 1856, the

*Westminster Kingsway Catering College*

museum successfully applied for a rent-free space in the new South Kensington Museum (later renamed the Victoria and Albert) which had been built with part of the profits from the Great 1851 Exhibition.

At first things went swimmingly at what were known as the "'Brompton Boilers" in South Kensington, until the museum ran short of money. The Government refused to restore the lost grant unless the museum allowed the Government to take over. The museum refused and the search for a new site started and eventually had a happy conclusion. At a meeting in Westminster Abbey's Jerusalem Chamber (where much of the King James Bible was written) a local stonemasonry company offered the museum a 30 year lease on premises in Bowling Street (later Tufton Street). The museum had come from one end of Thorney Island to Kensington and then back to the other end of Thorney Island.

The museum was initially financed by local contributions of money and donations of materials. The most curious was what Sir Charles Barry received from the Lucas brothers - six 50-foot-span iron supports from the 1862 Exhibition building in Kensington (not the famous 1851 one) for the basic frame of the Museum building and window casements. In addition, supplies of Caen stone and steel shutters were proffered by local suppliers.

Mark Liebenrood adds that in keeping with its original educational purpose, a school for architectural drawing was opened in 1870 and although money continued to be a problem the school did well and by the 1880s it had 200 students. It was, he says, "effectively subsidising the museum and changed its name to Westminster School of Art in 1890." Its alumni included Aubrey Beardsley, David Bomberg, Duncan Grant, H M Bateman (who wrote The Man Who cartoons) and Emily Carr.

Bateman described it in 1903 as "... arranged on four floors with galleries running round a big square courtyard, the whole being covered over with a big glass roof. Off the galleries were the various rooms which made up the school, the galleries themselves being filled with specimens of architecture which gave the whole place the air of a museum, which of course it was."

In 1904, the art school moved to Vincent Square to merge with the Westminster Technical Institute established with the help of Angela Burdett-Coutts. It consisted of a Civil Engineering academy and a Cookery academy. The School of Hospitality and Culinary Arts was founded in 1910 as part of the Technical Institute with the help of Escoffier and Cesar Ritz.

Meanwhile, in 1902, the Architectural Association took over the building and contents of the Royal Architectural Museum in Tufton Street. However, it had no long-term enthusiasm for the project and in 1916 it presented the bulk of its collections to the Victoria and Albert Museum (the V&A) where many of them can still be enjoyed today. The Westminster Kingsway Catering College is still flourishing today and the Westminster School of Art - which by 1931 had 654 students making it the largest art school in Middlesex - carried on until 1965 before moving to the West London College of Commerce in 1965. It says something about the fascinating growth of these organisations that all of them can trace their institutional DNA back to a shabby building in Canon Row on Thorney Island.

# 34: Should the Princes in the Tower really be the Princes in the Abbey?

The most famous person to claim sanctuary in Westminster Abbey was Elizabeth Woodville. She was a queen in her own right (wife of Edward IV), mother of another king (Edward the V, albeit uncrowned) and her daughter married yet another king (Henry VII) but it is for her stay on Thorney Island – where she twice took sanctuary to avoid prison during the Wars of the Roses – that she is chiefly remembered. Most famously when her husband Edward IV was forced to flee the country, she escaped from the Tower of London at night and claimed sanctuary twice in the Abbey on October 1st, 1470 and in April, 1483. She occupied rooms in the Dean's medieval quarters known as Cheyneygates. It is claimed to be the longest continuously occupied residence in London and still exists today. (see photo) The future King Edward V was actually born in the Sanctuary. Many kings have been buried in the Abbey precinct, but only one was born there

He became famous as one of the Princes in the Tower who were probably - but not definitely - murdered on the orders of Richard III who had both motive (getting rid of likely claimants for the throne) and opportunity, as they were both being held under his protection in the Tower of London.

Elizabeth was duped into letting her son leave the sanctuary during her second stay there in order to let him join his brother in the Tower of London, as dramatically told by Shakespeare in Richard III. It was on the spurious grounds that he would be looked after and that sanctuaries were for criminals not innocent children.

As the Duke of Buckingham put it to Cardinal Bourchier in Shakespeare's words:

"This prince hath neither claim'd it (sanctuary) nor deserv'd it,

And therefore, in mine opinion, cannot have it.

Then taking him from thence that is not there,

You break no privilege nor charter there.

Oft have I heard of sanctuary men,

But sanctuary children never till now."

Elizabeth eventually retired to the Royal apartments in Bermondsey Abbey in 1490 where she died two years later apparently destitute. She is buried beside her husband, Edward IV in St George's Chapel at Windsor.

Shakespeare's presumption that Richard III ordered the deaths of the two princes is coming under increasing scrutiny. It seemed to gain credence in 1674 when workmen discovered two small skeletons underneath a staircase in the Tower of London. King Charles II instructed that the bones be re-buried in Westminster Abbey where they still are today in the north aisle of the Henry VII Chapel. So, should we be talking about the 'Princes in the Abbey" not the Princes in the Tower?

The answer is not yet. The skeletons found in the Tower have a problematic provenance. An examination in 1933, which didn't have the benefit of modern techniques, could not determine the sex or exact age of the bones. Modern DNA testing would do better, but would need the permission of the Dean and Chapter of Westminster Abbey which is unlikely not least because

*Part of Cheynegates*

of fears it might open the door for a large number of other requests for disinterment. The opinion of King Charles III, to whom the Abbey reports, could make a difference, but his views are not known.

However, some fascinating research done by the team that discovered Richard III's remains in a Leicester car park, has produced interesting evidence that the princes escaped to the Continent. Philippa Langley, who led the Richard III discovery, presented new evidence in a Channel 4 documentary "The Princes in the Tower". This included a receipt for an army and weapons for an escaped Edward V and a document in an Austrian archive which depicted identifiable marks on the body of Edward's brother Richard, Duke of York. Critics claim that these and other bits of evidence could merely refer to the two known

pretenders, Lambert Simnel and Perkin Warbeck. Simnel, curiously, was pardoned by Henry VII after his failed rebellion and lived into the reign of Henry VIII. Warbeck was executed at Tyburn on November 23, 1499.

Philippa Langley suggests that DNA analysis could possibly identify one of the Princes in the Tower by comparing DNA from the bones held in the urn at Westminster Abbey with those of a known DNA relative of the prince who has been found, an approach that worked with Richard III. This 550 year real-life whodunnit continues.

# 35: The unsolved problem of the source of the Thames

It may seem ridiculous to include the River Thames as part of Lost London because everyone can see that it is there. Or is it? The only permanent part of what we see is the river bank and even that is slowly eroding over time in places. The Thames itself is rarely if ever the same water twice (unless, if after flowing out to sea, it evaporates into clouds and comes back again as rain).

*The "source" of the Thames at Kemble*

It emanates from a source that hasn't been agreed upon and the most popular candidate at Kemble (above) is problematic because it completely dries up during hot summers to become a lost river.

The Thames consists of fresh water - ignoring effluent from farms and other polluters - until Teddington Lock. It can then take anything from three weeks to three months for the water to reach the sea, depending on tides and other things.

A significant difference between water above and below Teddington is the amount of salinity in the water. Above Teddington the River contains fresh water, whereas below Teddington the water is salty, but the degree of salinity changes with the state of the tide and the volume of fresh water coming downstream. As fresh water is less dense than sea water, the fresh water forms a wedge and often moves out to sea flowing over the denser salt water. The tidal salt water can sometimes flow in a reverse direction below the fresh water.

However, as the tidal Thames is so irregular, (it zig zags through 25 sharp bends between Teddington and the sea), fresh and sea waters become thoroughly mixed and sometimes there is little difference between the salinity of the water at the surface and that near the bed. The overall salt content does gradually increase towards the sea, but the tidal Thames is essentially fresh water as far downstream as Battersea.

To understand London you have to travel outside - and what better place to start than the source of the Thames, without

The Thames by St Paul's Cathedral

which there would have been no river and no London. But where is the real source? The trouble is that when you do get to the supposed start of the Thames at Kemble, as mentioned above, during the parched summer season there is... nothing there. The Thames that you see flowing purposely past Thorney Island doesn't contain anything from its source for much of the year. This is also true of Thames Head a few miles north of Kemble which is recognised as the official source of the Thames by the Ordnance Survey. However, it also remains dry for much of the year in hot weather.

That leaves the third candidate, the River Churn, with a strong claim. It rises at Seven Springs in Gloucestershire and flows south for around 23 miles before it joins the Thames at Cricklade in Wiltshire. Unlike the other two source claimants,

Thames Head and Kemble, it flows throughout the year.

Since the distance from the source of the Churn to its confluence with the Thames is greater than that of the Thames from Kemble or Thames Head, it could be argued that the Churn is the source and the Thames merely its tributary,

This combined river would be eleven miles longer than the River Severn and so would qualify to be the longest river in the whole country, indeed maybe in the British Isles. This would be a bad blow for the River Severn but "Cricklade-on-Churn" would be in Seventh Heaven. However, "London-on-Churn"? It is difficult even to think about it, but it is still a fascinating curiosity that after well over a thousand years experts are still arguing where one of the most famous rivers in the world actually begins and what its name ought to be.

# 36: William Caxton, the man who changed the face of the English language

This unlikely spot on Thorney Island, taken from an 1850s photograph, has a fascinating history. The two buildings on the left - George Gilbert Scott's Crimea memorial column and his Gothic terrace, are still there today. The Royal Aquarium on the right which stretched down Tothill Street almost to St James's Park station is long gone, as is the 317 roomed Westminster Palace Hotel in the middle. It had the first hydraulic lifts in the country and was so close to the Abbey that it could almost touch it. It claimed to have a moderate tariff and no charge for "attendance", whatever that meant. Soon after it opened in 1860, the newly created India Office leased 140 rooms. For seven years until it moved into its permanent offices in Whitehall, the state of India was ruled from this hotel. At the time of writing, most of the site was known as 10 to 20 Victoria Street.

However, neither of these buildings were as revolutionary as what happened on the site of the hotel over 350 years earlier. It was then the Almonry where the monks of Westminster distributed alms to the poor. It was also where William Caxton (1422-1491) set up the first printing press in England. He didn't invent letterpress printing. That was the achievement of a German, Johannes Gutenberg in 1450. The Chinese had been doing it centuries earlier, but it was Gutenberg's invention which eventually swept the western world. It led to literature being mass produced rather than dependent on beautiful but laboriously produced scrolls, mainly by monks. It was the start of the information revolution.

Caxton revolutionised printing in Britain by enabling the bulk production of books and documents, but he also changed the shape and direction of the English language itself. This was because, having broken the monopoly of the monks over the written word - mainly religious tracts and usually not written in English - he had to decide which among all the dialects of England, he should choose as a standard so his books could be widely understood. He must have been tempted by his own Kent brogue, but he opted instead for something nearer to a London dialect.

Caxton himself pointed out the difficulty with a real life example of merchants stranded in the Thames for lack of wind. One of them asked at a house for 'eggs' only to be told by the "good wife" that she did not speak French. The merchant was annoyed because he could speak no French either, but happily one of his colleagues said they would have 'eyren' which the good wife understood. Happily the word eggs triumphed over eyren when Caxton's English ironed out many of the irregularities.

*The entrance to the hotel near where Caxton's house was situated*

John Timbs in his Curiosities of London (1855) says the precise site of Caxton's house was "immediately adjoining the spot now occupied by the principal entrance to the Westminster Palace Hotel". It was, he says, in Little Dean Street, on the north side of the Almonry backing against a house in Tothill Street. .

The hotel also had a statue of Caxton to remind itself of its heritage. No-one knows what happened to it, but it would be fitting if a new one were to be commissioned to honour one of Thorney Island's most influential sons. He is mainly remembered these days by Caxton Hall in nearby Caxton Street. It was once a celebrity wedding venue for a range of stars from Elizabeth Taylor to Ringo Starr, but is now a block of luxury apartments, albeit with an effigy of Caxton's head

among the literary busts running across the facade. Caxton deserves better.

*Caxton's house in the Almonry shortly before it was pulled down*

The picture of Caxton's house (above) is one of a number painted or engraved, but this one is unusual in having signs of bustling human activity. It also looks as though the house to the right of Caxton's, or possibly an extension of his own, had several windows bricked up to avoid the window tax which was still in operation when the drawing was done in 1827 (but not in Caxton's lifetime). The looming towers show how near it was to Westminster Abbey. Caxton was primarily a business man with skills in translation. Although he didn't invent printing he seized the opportunity of the new process with relish and helped England become part of a multimedia world. He had become interested in the new invention during his extensive travels on the Continent. He set up a printing press in Bruges where he translated and printed The History of Troy before bringing his printing press to Westminster in 1476, where he rented a loft over the Almonry gate until 1488 when, according to Dr Matthew Payne, Keeper of the Muniments at the Abbey, he ceased to rent the loft over the Almonry gate and took on a third and larger tenement in the precincts. Dr Payne says that Caxton's range as editor, translator, seeker of patronage, manager and marketer showed his flexibility but "he owed his commercial success less to the quality of his printing than to his strategy as a publisher."

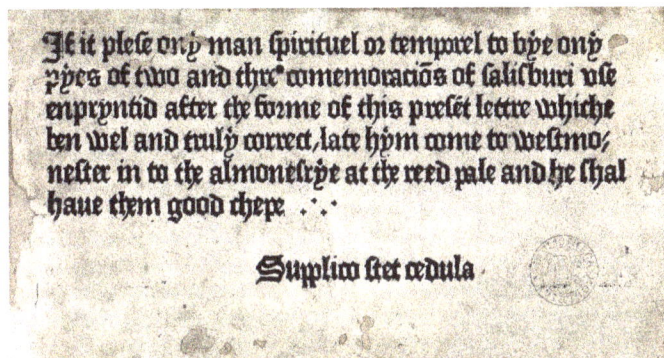

*The Brasenose College placard*

We know Caxton's main operations were in the Almonry partly because the library of Brasenose College in Oxford has an original placard (above) of Caxton's invitation to customers to "come to Westmonester into the Almonestrye, at the 'reed pale'", the name by which Caxton's House was known.

As a member of the 700-year old Mercers' Company, he would have been expected to to set up his business two miles away from Thorney Island in the City of London. Caxton thought better. He wanted to be near a potential source of demand, and so chose the precincts of Westminster Abbey where lawyers, aristocrats, politicians and clergy provided a ready market for the post-parchment printed word. Being located in Westminster meant he was free from all the petty regulations in the City. Caxton had a stall on a path leading to the Abbey on the eastern side where the back of the Chapter House (picture below) is today. Until recently it had a plaque on the wall, but his main operation was on two floors of the Almonry.

*The back of the Chapter House where Caxton had a stall*

To move from writing one-off scrolls to what became mass production with words printed in English not Latin or French, was truly revolutionary, akin to today's revolution in moving from analogue to internet-based digital.

The ability to mass produce meant that at the start there was a serious lack of what today would be called "content" which helps to explain why so many of Caxton's early books were either foreign or Anglicised versions of foreign publications.

Caxton was primarily a multi-media businessman who enabled knowledge to spread to ordinary people leading to a mass market for books, hitherto a monopoly of the monks. He wrote or translated countless thousands of words and is credited with being the first to use well over 1,000 new words in English. This may not be as dramatic an achievement as it sounds because so few books had been written in English before he set up shop, so it was relatively easy to introduce new words. He was responsible for more than a hundred editions, most of which were eventually in English, many translated by himself.

Caxton's first piece of printing in England was not a book, but an indulgence issued by Pope Sixtus in support of the war against the Turks. He got a fair amount of business from printing indulgences which, somewhat surprisingly, claimed to give Catholics relief from Hell or Purgatory in exchange for cash. This may help to explain why he started his business on Thorney Island where the potential market included monks used to producing religious scrolls, lawyers, royalty and aristocrats rather than traders in the City of London two miles away.

confederation. Others followed later. The tactical genius of the conference was Sir John Macdonald who later became the first prime minister of Canada.

In March 1867, the British North America Act received the Royal Assent of Queen Victoria in whose thoroughfare - Victoria Street - the conference had taken place. On 1st July 1867, the colonies of New Brunswick, Nova Scotia and the Province of Canada (today's Ontario and Quebec) were designated the Dominion of Canada.

The Westminster Palace Hotel was the scene of a counter-intuitive movement in 1908. The Women's National Anti-Suffrance League was formed in 1908 with the

*Caxton showing his printing to King Edward IV and his Queen*

The first book actually printed in England was The Game and Play of the Chesse which he translated from the French and published in 1474, but he soon turned to English. One of his earliest successes was Chaucer's The Canterbury Tales which is still in print over 550 years later.

In 1867, the Westminster Palace Hotel reached new political heights. It was the scene of a conference that created Canada as a country. It was the last of a series of conferences which brought the major regions of Canada into a single

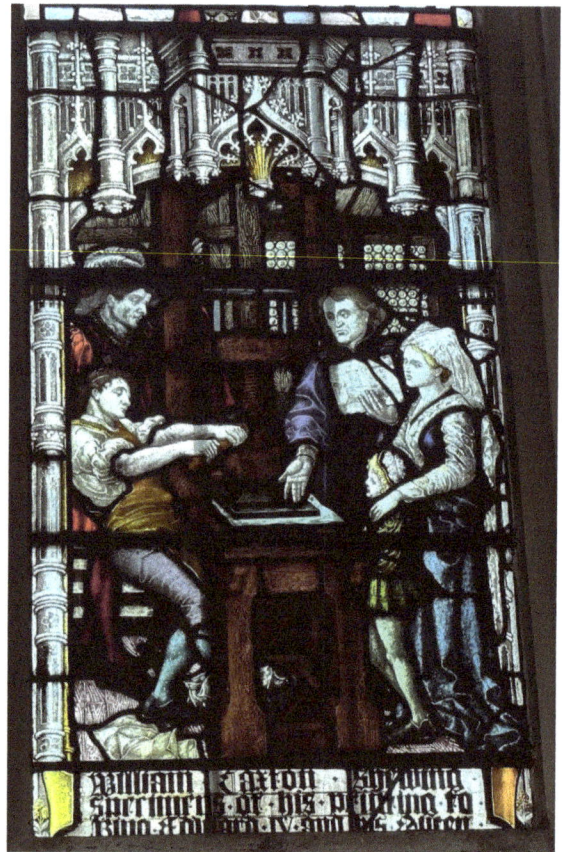

*Caxton was a churchwarden at St Margaret's where there is a stained glass window dedicated to him. He was buried at the church in 1479.*

*Wikipedia: The fathers of the Confederation meeting in the Conference Chamber of the Westminster Palace Hotel, 24 December 1866.*

aim of opposing women being granted the right to vote in parliamentary elections in the United Kingdom. Yes, you read that correctly, a group of women wanted to prevent women from having the vote in Parliamentary elections (though it would still be OK for women to vote in municipal elections). They felt the role of women was domestic rather than political. In 1910 it merged with the Men's National League for Opposing Women's Suffrage to form the National League of Opposing Women's Suffrage which, it has to be said, was not successful.

One has to be reminded with all these goings on that the Westminster Palace carried on as a hotel until it was closed in the 1920s and pulled down in 1974. It is difficult to imagine a hotel on such a prime site being demolished today. There are a lot of stories yet to be told.

In a BBC poll of the top 100 great Britons, William Caxton was placed 68th, just behind Tony Blair. He was just about the only business man on the list. He surely deserves a statue in view of his lasting influence on the development of printing and the shape of English in Britain. And where better than in part of the Almonry where he did so much of his work.

# 37: Henry V's secret rendezvous with an anchorite

The door to the right in the photograph above in the Chapel of St Benedict in Westminster Abbey, close by Poets' Corner, may well have changed the course of history. It was through this doorway that the Abbey's anchorite would pass to a life of seclusion, seldom to see the light of day again. He – or very occasionally she – would retire for a life of prayer and contemplation except for food deliveries and unusual occasions.

On one such occasion in March 1413, Henry V was mourning the death of his father Henry IV which took place in the nearby Jerusalem Chamber in the Abbey. He went to the anchorite secretly with the purpose of, as Shakespeare put it, "laying bare to him the secret sins of his whole life".

If Shakespeare is to be believed, the future Henry V, thinking his father had passed away, put the crown on his head in the Jerusalem Chamber only to be confronted by an angry father not yet dead. Was it this sin of pride that Henry V confessed to the anchorite? We will never know for he carried that secret with him to the grave but

it coincided with the new king turning his back on his roustabout life with Falstaff, as chronicled by Shakespeare, to turn himself into a model warrior king.

We know all about Henry V, but who was the anchorite? Dr Matthew Payne, Keeper of Muniments, who records the ownership of documents at the Abbey, recently unearthed his identity. He was John de London, presumably an assumed name, who was an anchorite at Westminster for an astonishing 40 years. Dr Payne says that the young Henry went to confess to de London on the night of his father's death under the cover of darkness. He would have been given penance to atone for his sins and probably spiritual advice that helped change the course of his life and our history - and Shakespeare's play

He was not the first king to consult an anchorite at the Abbey. During the Peasants' Revolt against the poll tax in 1381, Richard II

*The Jerusalem Chamber*

left the Tower of London to escape the violence in order to visit the shrine of Edward the Confessor at the Abbey, where he had his confession heard by the anchorite, a word that comes from the Greek word meaning "to withdraw". One of the most unusual anchorites was St Simeon Stylites – 390-459 – who apparently spent three years in a hut before establishing his dwelling on top of a 60 foot column.

What is left of the anchorage at Westminster is close to Poet's Corner. It is on the right hand side of the chapel of St Benedict, founder of the Benedictine order, which ran the monastery at Westminster until Henry VIII's dissolution in the 1530s. It had four stone walls with a window on to the Chapel so the occupant could partake in services. He would be served with food by an attendant, who would also deal with matters of personal hygiene.

The doorway to the Westminster anchorage which has a bust of a monk above it – presumably St Benedict –

was only rediscovered in 1878 during cleaning work, when a stone tablet was removed. The location of the cell had remained a mystery since being demolished at the dissolution of the monasteries. Dr Payne says that until the 14th century the anchorite's cell was located where the Jewel Tower is still standing. Even today you can still get an eerie feeling looking at this doorway to eternity.

# 38: The hidden gem of Parliament Square - St Margaret's church

*St Margaret's and the Abbey, almost joined together*

It took a long time for St Margaret's to become one of my favourite churches. It is perfectly positioned on Parliament Square, but hardly noticed by the millions of visitors each year, overwhelmingly from abroad, who visit Westminster Abbey which is literally a few yards away. It is as if a changeling child has been abandoned outside the Abbey for protection. If the Abbey wasn't there it would be a major destination in its own right. At present it is absent in plain sight - often empty when the Abbey is full - thereby concealing its fascinating history.

St Margaret's is very old. It was founded in the 12th century by the Abbey's Benedictine monks, ostensibly to give local people a church of their own. A more cynical view was that it was to keep the "lowlifes", which included lots of criminals seeking legally protected sanctuary in the vicinity of the Abbey, from disturbing their spiritual activities. The image below - drawn by Anton van den Wyngaerde in 1542 - shows that the area around St Margaret's (marked in yellow) had so many makeshift houses around it that it looked more like a shanty town. No wonder the monks wanted some peace and quiet.

*St Margaret's Church in 1542 surrounded by squat buildings*

We ought to give thanks that the church is there at all because there were two serious attempts to pull it down. In the 1540s, when Wyngaerde's drawing was made, the church was nearly destroyed – not by the Reformation or riots - but by the outrageous actions of one man, Edward VI's rapacious Lord Protector of England, Edward Seymour, the first Duke of Somerset. In order to build a palace on the Strand to match his ego, later called Somerset House, he set about destroying other buildings in order to seize their stone. They included part of the monastery of St John in Clerkenwell, the charnel house at St Paul's and the parish church near his proposed new building. He still hadn't got enough stone so he tried to pull St Margaret's down, but met his match. His workmen met fierce resistance from armed parishioners "with bows, arrows, staves and other such offensive weapons" according to a contemporary account. Somerset gave up. Justice later took its own revenge – he died before Somerset House was completed.

Seymour was arrested in 1551 and though acquitted of high treason was found guilty of felony for unlawfully assembling men in an attempt to incite insurrection which carried the death penalty. He was executed on 22nd January 1552.

The second attempt was strange in a different way. In 1840, a committee of the House of Commons criticised St Margaret's style of architecture on the grounds that it did not suit the Gothic nature of the Abbey. This was at a time when Gothic was all the rage as exemplified by the reconstruction of the Houses of Parliament after the 1834 fire in Gothic revival style. The MPs recommended unanimously that Saint Margaret's be dismantled stone by stone to be erected elsewhere. This plan was mercifully rejected, but the odd thing is why it was suggested in the first place given that since 1614, Saint Margaret's had been the official parish church of The House of Commons which was just across the road.

*Charles I looking across the road*

St Margaret's graveyard and its chapel at ease at Christchurch Gardens in Victoria Street have had their fair share of famous burials including William Caxton, Captain Blood, who nearly stole the Crown Jewels, the amazing black polymath Ignatius Sancho and his family, Wenceslas Hollar, the great engraver of London and many of the regicides who signed the death warrant of Charles I. This is referenced by St Margaret's with a touch of black humour. On the eastern wall of the church there is a small lead bust of Charles I looking across the road at a statue of his executioner Oliver Cromwell.

The most bizarre burial was that of Sir Walter Raleigh, a national hero, adventurer and in the end a convicted traitor, for being part of an alleged plot against James 1. He was executed in Old Palace Yard and then buried on the same day a hundred yards away under the altar of the Parliamentary church of St Margaret's at what must have seemed like a State funeral.

St Margaret's is unusual in that a large number of bodies are buried underneath, but there is not a single tomb above ground. Except for one. The only burial with a gravestone above ground is that of Alexander Davies, whose daughter Mary aged 12, married Sir Thomas Grosvenor, aged 21, a little-known baronet from the north of England in 1677. Mary brought with her a large acreage of land in London thought to be useless at the time, but which later became Mayfair and Belgravia. The land has been in the Grosvenor family ever since and could have made her, after adjusting for inflation over the years, Thorney Island's first billionaire.

St Margaret's, which is very much a working church, has had its fair share of fashionable marriages, including those of Samuel Pepys and John Milton in the 17th century and Winston Churchill and Harold Macmillan in the 20th. Pepys has left a record of one of his visits which is reproduced in the souvenir guide to the church. On 26th May 1667, he records that he "did entertain myself with my perspective glass (used to magnify images) up and

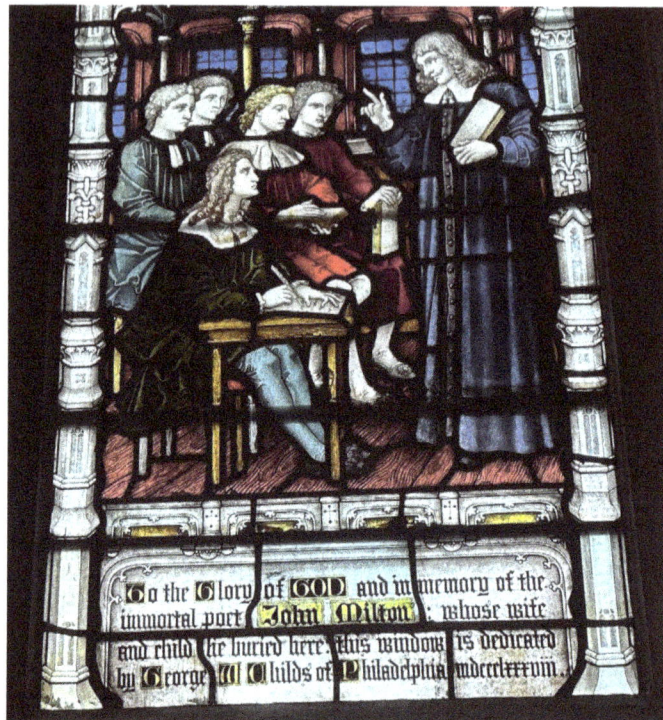

*John Milton dictating part of Paradise Lost*

down the church, by which I had the great pleasure of seeing and gazing at a great many fine women: and what with that and sleeping, I passed away the time till the sermon was done". It looks as though for Pepys this acted as the equivalent of a modern dating app.

One of the unforgettable things about St Margaret's is its stained glass. You won't get a more dramatic contrast than between John Piper's softly toned modernist windows along the right hand side as you go in and the amazing east window, which is a history lesson in itself.

This magnificent window with its sky blue background was finished around 1526 at Gouda in Holland and intended as a gift from the magistrates of Dort to Henry VIII to honour his marriage to Catherine of Aragon, both of whom are featured on the left and right at the bottom of the window which highlights the crucifixion of

Christ. However, in the years it took to make the window, circumstances changed. Henry ditched Catherine for Ann Boleyn, so the window had to be disposed of. But how? It was dispatched on an ecclesiastical version of pass-the-parcel to various destinations in Essex. It was hidden in as many as ten churches and private homes in Essex.

At first, it was dispatched to the ancient religious house of Waltham Abbey in Essex to be out of sight and out of mind. There it remained until the Dissolution of the Monasteries when it became a double embarrassment because of its association with a doomed Royal marriage and the imagery of a discarded Catholic religion.

Somehow it survived and was transferred to a private chapel at New Hall in Essex where its Catholic symbolism would be less noticed. It then came into the ownership of General Monk, a Royalist who also served with distinction under Cromwell, who apparently buried it to hide it from fanatical Puritans.

It was subsequently purchased by Edward Conyers of Copped Hall in Essex where Mary Tudor was imprisoned and where Shakespeare's A Midsummer Night's Dream is said to have been first performed. Its Cook's Tour continued when Conyer's son sold it in 1758 to the parishioners of St Margaret's for 400 guineas.

Then it starts getting complicated. The Dean and Chapter of Westminster regarded it as Popish imagery and started a lawsuit seeking its removal. The dispute lasted seven years. It was the religious equivalent of Charles Dickens' perpetual law suite in Bleak House, Jarndyce v Jarndyce. Fortunately for us all, the law suite failed and the stained glass window can now be enjoyed by all, hopefully in perpetuity.

St Margaret's is also linked with the extraordinary success of two black men who emerged from a background of slavery at a time of widespread illiteracy to become eminent men of letters and abolitionists in the latter part of the 18th century. Olaudah Equiano, who wrote a

*The much travelled east window*

page-turning bestseller about his experiences as a slave, is commemorated by a plaque inside the church where he was baptised. Ignatius Sancho, who was married in St Margaret's, is buried with his family in St Margaret's burial ground in Christchurch Gardens, Victoria Street. His letters, published posthumously, were subscribed to by a dizzy list of aristocrats, led by the Prime Minister Lord North – a fascinating case of Black Lives mattering over 250 years ago.

# 39: Richard the Lion-heart, King of a country he barely knew

There has been no King of England like Richard the Lionheart - or Cœur de Lion - and there never will be again. He was born and lived for only a short time in England. He was brought up in Aquitaine where he mainly spoke French and Occitan, the old Provencal language favoured by the troubadours. There is some doubt whether he spoke English at all. His statue is now resident in Old Palace Yard (above) on Thorney Island as a symbol of all things heroic and English though the truth is more complicated.

Richard the Lionheart is the only king not to have a number after his name in popular usage. In fact he was Richard l, a leading light during the Crusades. He is reckoned to have spent barely six months in England during his entire reign from 1189 until his death in 1199.

He gained a lasting reputation in England because of his success during the Crusades. He won several victories against his Muslim counterpart Saladin and although he failed in his aim of taking Jerusalem, he negotiated a deal that would keep access to the Holy Land in the hands of Crusaders for another century.

This made him a hero among Christians during a strongly religious age, but a modern more secular approach balances his undoubted victories abroad with his neglect of governance at home, not least the persecution of the Jews, that occurred during his reign.

The strangest, almost unbelievable, part of his reign was in 1192 when he was captured on his return from the Third Crusade. His ship was forced to stop near

*Richard the Lionheart being anointed during his coronation in Westminster Abbey*

Vienna where he was recognised despite disguising himself as a Knight Templar. Duke Leopold, who captured him, eventually handed him over to Henry VI, the Holy Roman Emperor, who demanded an unholy ransom for his release. The ransom demanded was 150,000 marks. Adjusting for inflation over the years is often problematic but the ransom in today's

money has been estimated by some - wait for it - to have been an astonishing £2.52 billion, equivalent to approaching three times the entire annual income of the Crown, a mind-boggling demand which it is difficult to believe. Richard was held in custody for 14 months until the ransom was paid. He was released on February, 1194,

The money was raised through selling assets including church property plus higher taxes on clergy and laity led by his mother, Eleanor of Aquitaine. The Crown also imposed special taxes and sold official positions and rights to lands and privileges.

The population of England during the time of Richard the Lionheart, around the late 12th century, is estimated to have been between 1.5 and 2 million people. If it was two million the cost of the ransom would have been £1,260 on average for each person, an unbelievable amount, even though the rich would have been paying much more. It nevertheless placed an enormous burden on poor people who often only earned a few pence a day if that. It left a lasting antagonism towards increased taxation which affected England right up to the Peasants Revolt of 1381.

Richard died in 1199, killed by an arrow fired by a former friend Bertram de Gurdun, also known as Pierre Basile, who wrongly claimed Richard had killed his father and brothers. Whether for this reason or something else Richard forgave him before he died, an act that is commemorated in a horizontal sculpture beneath the equestrian statue outside Parliament.

The statue itself, created by the Italian sculptor Baron Carlo Marochetti, has a bit of history of its own which is described on Wikipedia as follows:

"It was first produced in clay and displayed at The Great Exhibition of 1851 in Hyde Park outside the west entrance to what became known as the Crystal

*Richard, Coeur de Lion, at the Great Exhibition of 1851*

depicted an unworthy subject – "a disobedient son and a bad governor".

The statue eventually found its way to Old Palace Yard after £640,000 (in today's money) had been raised by private donations and other locations such as Buckingham Palace, Hyde Park and Marble Arch had been rejected. The Lionheart still stands proud in Old Palace Yard even though one can't get close to him as he is part of the car park of the House of Lords.

Intriguingly, a rival post-modern sculpture, a riff on the original, has sprung up a few hundred yards away in Orchard Place off Victoria Street. Created by the sculptor Nick Hornby, it depicts Richard as a romantic warrior on one side but as you walk around it mutates into what looks like a war machine, enabling viewers to read what they like into the reputation of this enigmatic monarch.

Palace where it received a mixed reception not least because its tail fell off the day after it was installed. Queen Victoria and Prince Albert headed a list of illustrious subscribers to raise money for the casting of the statue in bronze but others wondered why the warlike figure of the Lionheart should be symbolising an event like the Great Exhibition which was designed to bring nations together."

The influential art critic John Ruskin said of the model, "it will tend more to educate the public with respect to art than anything we have done for centuries". The Art Journal, however, argued that the statue was merely a novelty and, worse,

*Richard the Lionheart with 55 Broadway in the background*

# 40: The Abbey's 700 year-old garden

*The medieval garden*

Most people walking along Abingdon Street towards Millbank - opposite the Houses of Parliament - have no idea that the wall on the right which continues around the corner into Great College Street (where the remains of the Tyburn River may still flow underneath) is the actual medieval wall that guarded the monastery. It also hides one of the hidden gems of London.

If you are outside it is difficult to believe that on the other side of the wall is the oldest continuously cultivated garden in the country reaching back at least to 1297: yet once inside it is so serenely calm that it

is difficult to believe that the rest of the world carries on outside. According to Jan Pancheri, who recently retired as head gardener - and has written a book The Gardens of Westminster Abbey - it has a microclimate that is two degrees higher than outside.

Asked what makes the garden unique, Jan says: "There's a real sense of the sacred, with a great feeling of quietness and respect. It's an open contemplative space where you can have your own thoughts." She adds that they have arranged plants that the monks would have used such as wildflowers, aromatic plants, and vegetables like cabbages and onions to make the place pleasant.

Sitting in the garden behind the walls you don't see the bustle of London, just the legacy of history; the Chapter House, the towers of the Abbey and the upper reaches of the buildings of Parliament.

Wandering around the lawn, it is easy to imagine what it once contained. There was an orchard, a dovecote, a cider mill, (plus a still for distilling waters from herbs) two ponds, fruit and vegetables and even a tiny vineyard plus a herbarium which the Abbey has records of going back to 1297. The main reason for the garden's creation was for the College's infirmerer to provide medicinal herbs for the monks and there is still a herbarium on roughly the same site. There used to be a channel nearby leading from the monks' "reredorter" to a mill at the southern edge of the garden by the Thames, from which the word Millbank is derived. In case you are wondering about the word "reredorter" it comes from the Anglo-French words "rere" meaning "behind" and "dorter" meaning dormitory. Geddit? OK, let's stick to "necessarium" in Latin or just latrines in plain English.

*What is left of the reredorter is at the end of the cloister walk*

The dimensions of the garden are unchanged from medieval times except that King Edward III (1312-1377) seized part of the north eastern end to provide more room for his palace and the Jewel Tower he was building.

If you were to dig in the garden you would soon be unearthing the deposits which formed Thorney Island. Today's garden has a fig tree, plane trees that were planted in 1850 and two handsome mulberry trees (one black, one white) at each end of the garden. Either side of the stone gateway leading to Little Dean's Yard (part of Westminster School) there were, until recent years, two stone angels, reputably made by Grinling Gibbons and Arnold Quellin, which once graced a Chapel at the other end of Whitehall Palace where the Ministry of Defence building now is. Even in their worn condition they were a magical presence. Hopefully, they have been taken away temporarily for restoration.

*The statues at the (private) entrance to Little Dean's Yard*

On the right of the photo is a stone pineapple, a traditional sign of hospitality above which can be viewed at the end of a grape vine which covers the neighbouring wall.

*An impressive statue, now gone, from the southern end of the garden*

Until recently, College Garden and the Chapter House were open to the public for free but the Abbey has stopped this commendable practice because visitors were telling each other on the internet, how to use the benefit of free access to creep into the main Abbey for nothing instead of (at the time of writing) paying £30 for a ticket. This is understandable from the Abbey's point of view since it doesn't get any significant grants from the Government and has huge costs to keep the infrastructure of the Abbey intact. Well over 90% of the Abbey's income comes from visitors mainly from overseas. However, it is surely not beyond the wit of man or God to crack down on interlopers to allow access to people seeking tranquility in the garden without having to pay £30 each time.

The garden is of great significance not only because it is still there, but because the Abbey's library has preserved an amazing number of documents chronicling the plant life of the garden back to 1298 which have been gathered together in The Infirmerer's Garden by John H Harvey published by The Gardens Trust. A typical example of this is that we know, for instance, that in 1310 a man was hired for three days to repair the vines and another to plant leeks in 1321 at a cost of 14d. One can't help thinking that it is highly unlikely that the so-called information revolution will preserve such detailed events of everyday life hundreds of years hence.

# 41: The astonishing Duchess of Newcastle

*The Cavendish tomb hemmed in between British politicians*

If you go into Westminster Abbey from the tourists' entrance on Parliament Square, there is a tomb on the left that nearly everyone misses unless it is drawn to their attention. It is the tomb of the Duke of Newcastle who was a commander in Charles I's army during the civil war and who was awarded a dukedom later on by Charles II. What is unusual about the tomb is that the Duke's wife, the extraordinary Margaret Cavendish, is raised to a slightly higher level than her husband - at the request of the Duke himself who oversaw the design by Grinling Gibbons. She is holding an open book and an ink pot to highlight her literary achievements which have only started to be appreciated in recent years.

Margaret Cavendish has been rightly described by Professor Peter Sherlock as "one of the most astonishing women of the 17th century". At the time she was dismissed as eccentric and nick-named "Mad Madge", but in recent years her contributions to science, poetry, plays, essays and feminism are seen to have been way ahead of their time despite her lack of formal schooling.

Her eccentricities included requiring her footman to sleep in a closet in her bedroom so he could be summoned to write down any thoughts she had during the night.

And she certainly had a lot of thoughts. She eventually produced ten volumes of what have been described as "learned trifles and fantastic verses" many of which were so short they may have come straight from her footman's notes, but which are now being examined by academics for signs of deep insights.

She often sent copies of her work to distinguished people, sometimes receiving extravagant praise from the recipients, possibly with their tongues in their cheeks.

The Duchess undoubtedly suffered from being a woman at a time when the scientific establishment didn't take women seriously, but she had also married into the Cavendish scientific dynasty. This may help to explain why she was invited to attend a meeting of the all-male Royal Society in May 1667, despite protests from many of the fellows. It was a couple of centuries before the experiment was repeated.

Pepys, who was there, recorded in his diary that her dress was "so antic and her deportment so unordinary" that the fellows were made strangely uneasy. They would be, wouldn't they…

But what was thought silly then, mainly by men, is looked at differently today. She was a prolific author and an early feminist who published poems, plays,

The Duchess, book in hand, lying slightly higher than her devoted husband

literary critiques and volumes of what are today highly thought of observations and works on natural science. She wrote numerous poems, some with a scientific bent, including A warr with Atomes which explored the nature of matter. At a time of widespread ignorance of the nature of matter Cavendish used poetry to help explain it:

"Small atoms of themselves a world may make,

For being subtle, every shape they take.

And as they dance about, they places find;

Of forms, that best agree, make every kind.

After returning to London from exile in Paris with her husband following the Restoration, the Duchess became a prolific author. She produced ten volumes of what have been described as "learned trifles and fantastic verses", many of which were so short they might have come straight from her footman's notes. She also wrote plays, one of which, The Humourous Lovers, was described by Samuel Pepys in 1667 as "the most silly thing that ever came upon a stage".

But what was thought silly then is looked at differently today. Cavendish was an early feminist whose poems, plays and literary critiques are nowadays pored over for signs of deep insights. Her observations about natural science are today highly thought of.

Her book, The Blazing World, is thought to be the first work of science fiction by a woman and a pioneer of the genre itself.

During the English Civil War (1642-1651), the Royalist Duke and Duchess of Newcastle fled from the wrath of Oliver Cromwell, first to Paris and then, for 12 years, to Antwerp where they rented the house of Rubens from his widow. The Duchess published several works during their sojourn in Antwerp including: Natures Pictures (1656), Sociable Letters (1664), and The World's Olio which contains references to local Antwerp life.

Throughout her time in Antwerp, Margaret Cavendish appears to have used the Rubens House as a base for her literary, social, and cultural activities, engaging with local people and English exiles while developing her skills as a writer and patron of the arts.

A long article in the Stanford Encyclopedia of Philosophy admits that though Cavendish's philosophical work was not taken seriously in the 17th

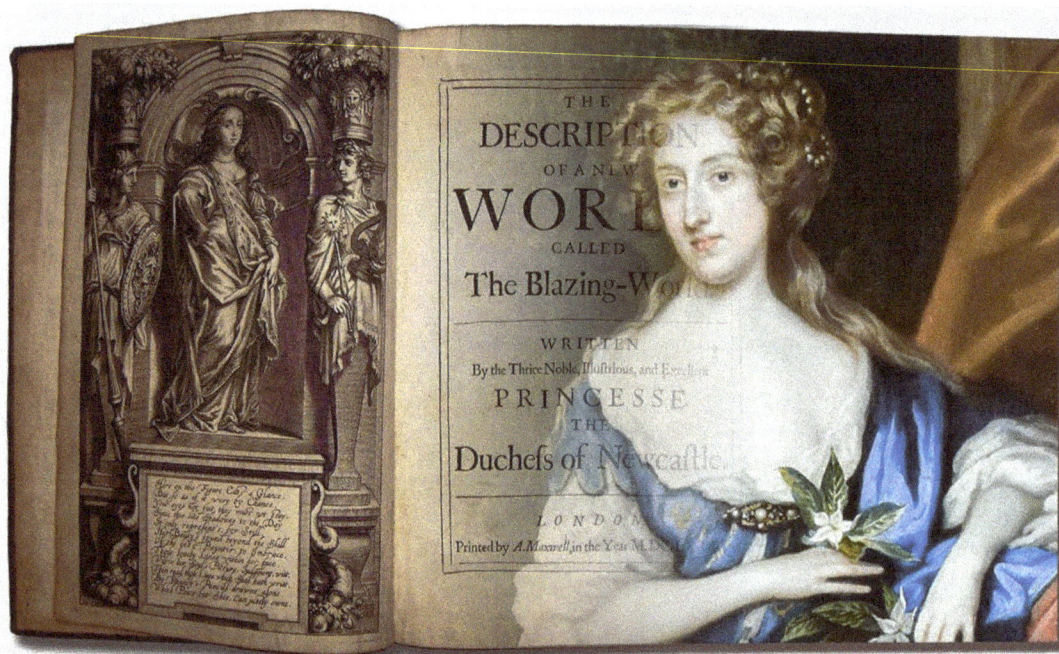

*Margaret in front of The Blazing World (Wikipedia)*

*Rubens' house in Antwerp*

century "it is certainly relevant today". The Duchess, it claims, laid out "an early and very compelling version of the naturalism that is found in current-day philosophy and science". Among numerous other things she offered important insights that are relevant to recent discussions of the nature and characteristics of intelligence.

The encyclopedia adds that she "anticipated some of the central views and arguments that are more commonly associated with figures like Thomas Hobbes and David Hume".

# 42: In memory of Philip Clark, plumber

Westminster Abbey is celebrated for the great and the good who are buried or memorialised there from kings and queens of England to the great physicists Isaac Newton and Stephen Hawking. So it is as welcome as it is surprising to find that over 300 years ago, an ordinary plumber, Philip Clark, was buried there - and not as one name on a long list, but with a large tombstone of his own. It was one of the largest in the main cloister and set in white rather than the usual black marble. Very little is known about him. He was much too early to have been involved with the more famous, but unmemorialised, plumber, Thomas Crapper (1836 - 1910), a surprising amount of whose work can be seen around the Abbey.

Christine Reynolds, assistant keeper of the Muniments at the Abbey, says: "It was usual for Abbey workmen to be buried in the cloisters at this period, and have the normal size of gravestone for the time. The stone must have been re-cut at some time to be still clear enough to read".

Clark was not married, apparently, and left his estate to Frances Warren, his sister's child, having worked at the Abbey doing lead and pipe work around the Abbey and at Westminster School for 43 years until his death in 1707. As a plumber, Clark would almost certainly have been involved in the maintenance of the conduit the monks built to take water from the Tyburn river.

An American plumber, whose mother was called Clark, was bowled over on seeing, during a recent visit, that one of his profession was honoured over 300 years ago in one of the most famous churches in the world. He went away hoping to find that he was related to him.

Although the burial of workmen in the Abbey appears to have been not uncommon in those days, it is excellent that the Abbey has preserved this tombstone as a fitting memory of ordinary folk. It doesn't compare with the tomb of the unknown warrior. Its real significance is as a reminder of the thousands of workmen who toiled anonymously to help make the Abbey what it is today.

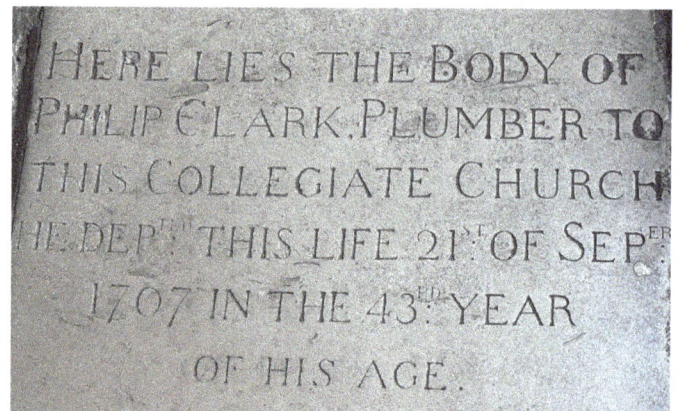

HERE LIES THE BODY OF PHILIP CLARK. PLUMBER TO THIS COLLEGIATE CHURCH HE DEP.'D THIS LIFE 21.st OF SEP.er 1707 IN THE 43.rd YEAR OF HIS AGE.

# 43: Ministering to the necessities of life

This corner of the Abbey's Little Cloister is hardly noticed by any of the large numbers of visitors to the Abbey, and is a bit of a puzzle even if you do notice it. The tiles at the top suggest that whatever it was must have been quite tall. In fact it is almost all that remains of a vital bit of 11th century engineering, built at the time of Edward the Confessor, that changed the life of the monks at Westminster.

It goes back to St Benedict (AD 480- AD 547), the founder of the Benedictine order. He laid down that the period after morning matins was reserved for the "necessities" of life. The place where the necessities of life were performed was usually located behind the dorter (Latin for dormitory). It became known as using the reredorter ("rere" is French for "behind"), one of the more obscure euphemisms of its kind.

The fact remains that for all their otherworldliness, the monks needed to come down to earth and spend a penny before washing themselves. Hence this two-storey structure which supplied water from a conduit built in Hyde Park travelling along sunken wooden pipes - some of which are still there - under St James's Park and Strutton Ground, and then between the kitcheners' garden and the Almonry at the entrance to the Abbey (where money was distributed to the poor) and into the monastery itself. It flowed through the reredorter by the side of the Little Cloister before exiting into the Thames through a drain, the remains of which can still be seen by the Jewel Tower. If you had walked in the other direction - i.e. through the blocked wall in the photo - you would have come to Little Dean's Yard and the ancient Ashburnham House, both of which have remnants of the reredorter, but are now part of Westminster School.

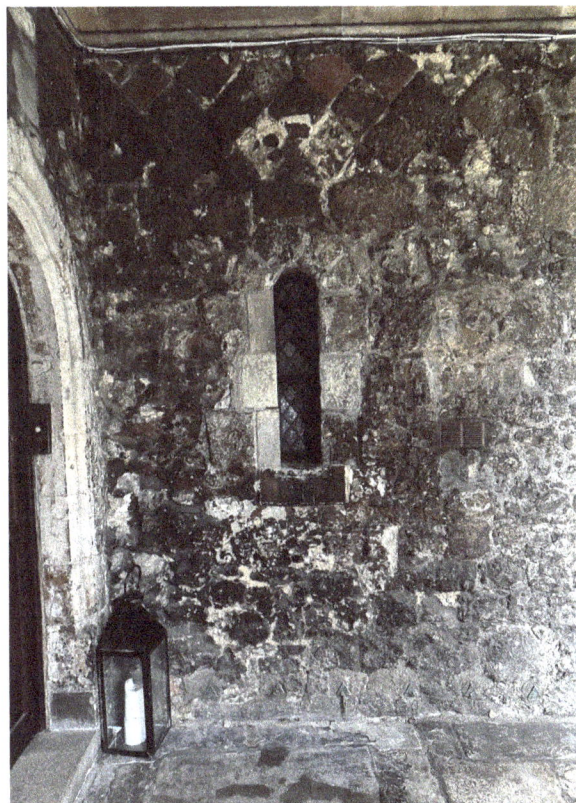

*The intriguing reredorter*

The reredorter was 96 feet long by 30 feet wide. It consisted of two storeys with the latrines situated on the upper level. The photo shows barely half of the height of it. There was a deep drop into stone lined sewers below so that... let's not go there.

The reredorter meant that the monks had access to fresh, or freshish, water that was not available to the general population. However, the Grand Conduit in New Palace Yard, which lasted from the 15th to the 17th century, was a secular fountain open to local inhabitants for their water supplies.

# 44: A journey into virtual reality

Westminster Abbey is a mesmerising medieval church, yet it can also be viewed as a museum of sculptures with a unique church attached. There are around 600 monumental sculptures which the huge number of visitors who pass by can only partially absorb.

The most eye-catching sculptor has to be Louis François Roubiliac (1702-62), a brilliant Frenchman who moved to London to find fame, fortune and, like so many creatives of the era, eventual poverty.

His most dramatic work - an 18th century foray into virtual reality - depicts Lady Elizabeth Nightingale, who died in pregnancy, with her husband forlornly trying to fend off the skeletal figure of Death which has risen from the depths of the underworld, deathly spear in hand. In real life, she was killed by a bolt of lightning which not even a great sculptor like Roubiliac could reproduce in stone.

It was an attempt to rewind history so that Elizabeth's husband Joseph Gascoigne could be seen vainly to be trying to prevent Death from taking his wife. The sculpture was carved of white Carrara marble from north Tuscany that has been used for a huge number of monuments, from Michelangelo's David to the Marble Arch in London. The Carrara quarries are said to have produced more marble than any other place on earth.

Washington Irving, the American author of Rip Van Winkle (actually written while he was in Birmingham, England) said it was 'among the most renowned achievements of modern art'. John Wesley, one of the founders of Methodism, observed that it was one of the finest monuments in the Abbey, because "the marble seems to speak".

Maybe it was the marble's supposed speech that was behind the story of a robber who broke into the church, but was so frightened by the shadowy figure of Death that he fled in terror.

# 45: Uncovering the Grand Sacristy among the sands of Thorney Island

*The original sand of Thorney Island in the Grand Sacristy*

One of the fascinating things about Westminster Abbey is that fresh bits of its buried history are still being uncovered by archaeologists. One of the latest is Henry III's Great Sacristy between the Abbey and St Margaret's churchyard which, when it is reconstructed, will be a new welcoming place for visitors to the Abbey built on some of its medieval remains. It has been renamed the King Charles III Sacristy.

The excavations were started by Sir Gilbert Scott way back in 1869, when the ground level had to be reduced by up to three feet to remove the centuries of accumulation.

In the cloister area near the Sacristy, a large Roman sarcophagus with a lid dating back to the 4th century was found. It can now be seen in the Triforium museum, upstairs in the Abbey.

In 2009, the Abbey invited Channel 4's Time Team to conduct an exploratory excavation. This confirmed that the foundations of the L shape building were intact along with other well-preserved archaeological deposits. Recent excavations by Pre-Construct Archaeology have unearthed more remains of the sacristy built in the 1250s by Henry III, at his own expense. This was part of his complete reconstruction of Edward the Confessor's 11th-century church remnants of which were found, including dozens of bodies, presumed to be mainly monks.

During the excavations a "stacked grave" was uncovered which at first was thought to have belonged to the "regicides" who participated in the execution of Charles I. However, later analysis of the dates showed this was not possible, though some of the regicides were buried nearby in the churchyard of St Margaret's. They had been exhumed from their original burial places in the Abbey on the orders of Charles II to avenge the death of his father, Charles I.

More intriguingly, at least for me, was something else. While archaeologists were digging underneath the surface they found what an official guide told us during a visit was "the original sand of Thorney Island" (pictured above). It was typical of the sand and gravel that enabled the formation of what became Thorney Island, one of the few islands or eyots in the Thames floodplain, to be formed higher than the surrounding marshland. This made it habitable for the original monastery and Abbey and with less flooding risk. Without this gift of nature there would have been no Abbey or Royal Palace in that place, let alone a Thorney Island.

# 46: Where Henry Purcell and Robert Herrick plied their trade

*St Ann's Lane with Purcell's house on the right drawn on April 15, 1845 by R W Withal*

St Ann's Lane always was, and still is, a short narrow thoroughfare leading from Old Pye Street to Great Peter Street in Westminster. It achieved notoriety in the 19th century when, along with Old Pye Street, it was the epi-centre of degradation and criminality that Charles Dickens popularised as "The Devil's Acre".

Much less well known is that in the late 17th century it had seen better days. It was the home of two giants of English culture. On 10th September 1659, Henry Purcell, one of the greatest of all English composers, was born in St Ann's Lane in the house pictured above. It is where St Andrew's youth club, claimed to be the oldest in the world, is located today. One of the existing residents was the poet Robert Herrick and they must have overlapped for a while. Herrick's most remembered words are::

"Gather ye rose-buds while ye may,

Old Time is still a-flying;

And this same flower that smiles today

Tomorrow will be dying."

This was but one of 2,500 poems he wrote, half of which were released in a single major collection, Hesperides, published in 1648, on his return to his native London from Devon. Herrick apparently expected the book to be read in its entirety in the order in which it was printed.

Herrick and Purcell were there at the same time for barely three years, but Herrick must have been aware of a newborn baby in such a tiny street, not least because he was a clergyman. He had been forced to leave his parish at Dean Prior in Devon when the Puritans took over during the English civil war to return to his beloved London for 13 years.

Bust of Henry Purcell in Christchurch Gardens, Victoria Street, Westminster

Herrick had to rely on the charity of some of his wealthy friends in London, where he was born, after he had lost his income as a clergyman in Devon. He was a big fan of Ben Jonson and was in one of the literary circles known as the Sons of Ben.

On 24th August 1662, after the restoration of the monarchy, Herrick left St. Ann's Lane to resume his clerical duties at Dean Prior. He died in 1674 aged 83 when Purcell, a child prodigy, would have been 15. Although they would never have had a conversation, it is fascinating that two masters of their craft lived for a short while in the same tiny street, which later became a source of degradation and iniquity.

Had they been true contemporaries, they would have had plenty to talk about as dozens of Herrick's poems were set to music in the 17th century, not least by William and Henry Lawes who apparently performed their version of Herrick's What Sweeter Music before King Charles I at Whitehall. It includes the lines

"Dark and dull night, fly hence away,

And give the honour to this day,

That sees December turned to May".

Neither Purcell nor Herrick are household names today, but both are still remembered over 350 years later. Purcell still has a global reputation among classical music lovers and is played around the world, while Herrick's words are still quoted even though the source may not be apparent. There is a Herrick Street near Tate Britain. Purcell has no street but has a formidable bust in Christchurch Gardens, Victoria Street.

The words of Charles Burney, an 18th century historian, still resonate today. Purcell, he said, "is as much the pride of an Englishman in music as Shakespeare in productions of the stage, Milton in epic poetry, Locke in metaphysics or Sir Isaac Newton in philosophy and mathematics". Modernists influenced by Purcell include Stanley Kubrick (in the 1971 film A Clockwork Orange), Jethro Tull and Pete Townsend of The Who.

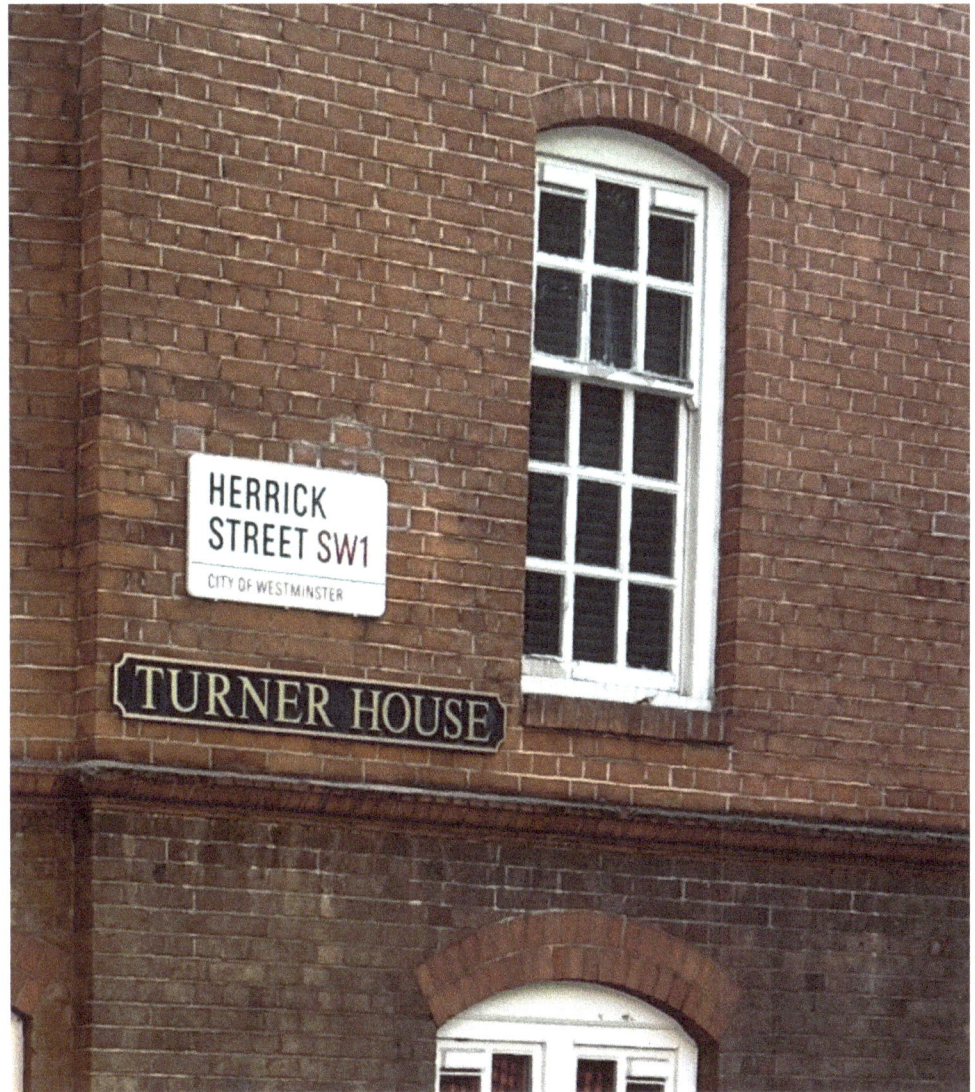

# 47: They died in poverty

Oh, rare Ben Jonson,
As should be known
by every London cabbie,
He's buried standing up
in Westminster Abbey.
(VK)

It is very sad to look at the roll call of some of Britain's most revered poets buried at Poet's Corner and to be reminded how many died in poverty. The saddest of all was Ben Jonson, who in his latter years lived in a house in the Abbey grounds close to St Margaret's Church, but who, despite a glittering career writing plays and masques for royalty as well as the ordinary folk of London, died in what was called "Greek Poverty" or utter penury.

A proper grave was beyond his means and he ended up being buried, at his own request, standing up. It is the only instance of a vertical burial in the Abbey taking up a minimal amount of the Abbey's precious space. He may have been a bit ahead of his time as the problem of London running out of burial space could have been solved if all tombs were vertical rather than horizontal.

The tile that marks his grave can be seen on the left after entering the western entrance to the Abbey near a plaque on the wall with the famous words "O rare Ben Johnson" (the original spelling). Whether he or someone else wrote the words and whether there should be no space between the first two letters (which would turn it into the Latin 'orare' meaning to pray), a possible allusion to Jonson's Catholic leanings, is still a matter for discussion. The words were apparently suggested by a passer by who paid a workman to carve the epithet.

*Ben Jonson*

The next day the chasm between poverty and fame was closed when Jonson was interned after a procession attended according to a contemporary by "all or the greatest part of the nobility and gentry then in the town".

This same bizarre ritual attended the funerals of Edmund Spenser (or Spencer), author of The Faerie Queen, and Michael Drayton, a major poet and playwright. Both died in poverty only to be given what seemed like State funerals.

Spenser, according to his friend William Drummond

*Edmund Spenser*

of Hawthornden, died in real poverty "for the lack of bread" in King Street Westminster, yet soon after he died, aristocrats and poets alike came to shower laurels on his grave. His coffin was carried in state from his last home in King Street across today's Parliament Square to the Abbey paid for by the Earl of Essex. Then, according to William Camden, the historian, something happened that still resonates today. His hearse "was attended by poets and mournful elegies, and poems with the pens that wrote them were thrown into his tomb". Scholars still wonder whether Shakespeare was among the mourners and, if he was, could something he wrote still be there?

Michael Drayton, who is all but forgotten nowadays but was a rival to Shakespeare in his time, died in poverty on 23rd December 1631 at his lodgings in Fleet Street close by St Dunstan's church. Yet he was so highly regarded by his contemporaries that, according to the antiquary William Fulman: "The Gentlemen of the Four Innes of Court and others of note about the Town, attended his body to Westminster."

*Michael Drayton*

Geoffrey Chaucer, the first resident of Poets' Corner, may have avoided penury on his death but if so it was only just. In 1398, he was forced to borrow against his annuity and was sued for debt. However, in 1399, shortly before his death, Chaucer was granted an annual pension by King Henry IV, which would have secured his financial stability.

Wenceslaus Hollar (1607-1677) was not a poet but his amazing engravings of London leave us all in his debt, making him a match for the poets in terms of creativity. Like them he also died in abject poverty on Thorney Island in Gardener's Lane. His portfolio of engravings in England and Europe, many of them executed when he was a favourite of his long-term employer Lord Arundel, were an astonishing achievement, yet didn't prevent an ignominious death when he had to plead with the bailiffs in his room as a favour not to take his bed away before he died. He was buried in St Margaret's churchyard.

# 48: Merrie England arises in slum-torn Westminster

The area in front of City Hall in Victoria Street, now the site of an enormous office block, used to be one of the wonders of old Westminster. It was here in 1654 that a local philanthropist did something special. He built Palmer's Village, a romanticised memory of Merrie England complete with a village green, a pub, a blacksmith and even a maypole.

It was on the site (in yellow) where the Army and Navy Stores started life in 1871 as a cooperative selling a variety of goods to officers and others in the army. It was much loved by its customers, not least some of

Six almshouses above Palmer's Village (Horwood's Plan). The Devil's Acre is in red on the right (1792-79)

the characters in Agatha Christie novels. Many of its goods were manufactured in local factories and workshops. It was later taken over by the House of Fraser and then Sports Direct.

What made Palmer's Village remarkable was its location. To the east, barely a couple of hundred yards away, was the notorious Devil's Acre, a no-go area for police, full of criminals and prostitutes. It had an actual school for pickpockets, the idea for which was almost certainly pickpocketed by Charles Dickens as the model for the fictional Fagin's Den in Oliver Twist. Palmer's Village was built extremely close to the

ancient Bridewell Prison (where the Greencoat Boy pub is today) as the map below indicates.

The Bridewell was later replaced by a far bigger prison where Westminster Cathedral stands today. It wasn't an obvious place to recreate the myth of Merrie England hemmed in by prisons and slums, but it seems to have worked.

It was called Palmer's Village after the Rev. James Palmer who, along with other philanthropists attached to Thorney Island, built much needed almshouses and schools creating an impact which is still felt today. The map at the top of this article shows that six almshouses were built close to each other by philanthropists whose memories have been retained by the names of the roads.

The pioneer was Cornelius Van Dun (1483–1577), a Flemish soldier who, amazingly, served four monarchs (Henry Vlll, Edward, Mary and Elizabeth), quite a feat in those days, and died at the astonishing age of 94. Starting in 1569, he built 20 houses for poor widows at his own expense in Petty France, where Vandon Street is today and nearby St Ermin's Hill. The epitaph on his grave is the oldest in St Margaret's church.

Palmer built his village in order to provide long-term financial support for the almshouses he had constructed across the road in Palmer Street where the Albert pub is today.

Palmer's initiative was, astonishingly, one of six almshouses within hugging distance of each other. They were built by benefactors whose good works are remembered 350 years later today in nearby streets including Emery Hill Street, Vandon Street (named after van Dunn), Dacre Street and Palmer Street. Nicholas Butler also had a street named after him off Palmer Street near where his two almshouses were located.

Lady Dacre built the almshouses known as Emanuel Hospital in 1600 on the site of today's prestigious Taj Hotel in Buckingham Gate. Westminster City, a comprehensive school which backs on to the end of the Taj hotels, can trace its ancestry back to Lady Dacre's almshouses on the same piece of land.

1898.
Spring and Summer Fashions.
MANTLES, JACKETS, TEA GOWNS, SUNSHADES, LACE GOODS, &c.
No. 9 Dept.
Drapery.
The ARMY & NAVY Co-operative Society, Limited,
105, VICTORIA STREET, WESTMINSTER, S.W.

Cornelius van Dunn, pioneer of Westminster almshouses (from St Margaret's Church)

James Palmer in St Margaret's church

The Rev. Palmer (1595-1659) had Thorney Island written all over him. He was born in 1585 and was baptised and buried in St Margaret's Church. He spent much of his priesthood at St Brides in Fleet Street where he could often be found sleeping in the steeple to save money. He gave regular sermons at St Margaret's including to both houses of Parliament. He is remembered by plaques in the church and also high up in Rochester Row by the junction with Emery Hill Street, though you will have to strain your eyes to find it let alone read it.

By 1834, the Bridewell prison had been replaced by an enormous new penitentiary, the Tothill Fields prison which stretched from today's Francis Street to Victoria Street, on the land where Westminster Cathedral is today. It would have completely dominated the view from Palmer's village. The foundations of the prison were so strong they were retained. The Cathedral rests on the base of the former prison.

The 1841 census gives us an idea of the sorts of people who were living in Palmer's village. There were labourers, servants, brassworkers, a scavenger, a hat trimmer, a stonemason, a laundress, a stableman, a plasterer, a soldier and so on, a plausible cross section of Merrie England.

In 1853, Charles Manby Smith wrote a wonderful description of it called "A Deserted Village in London" known as Palmer's Village. He tells us that he had lived in the village during many happy years of his youth, some twenty or thirty years earlier. He deplored the way that the village had been swallowed up by the expansion of London and then disappeared altogether when Victoria Street was constructed through it between 1845 and 1851.

Smith wrote of "the great Babylon, where, though hemmed in all around by crowded streets, dark narrow lanes and fetid courts, it (Palmer's Village) yet retained many of the rural charms of its primal condition. It had yet a village green...and on the green, every first of May, up rose, reared by invisible hands in the night, the village May-pole, round which we have seen the lads and lasses dancing to the music of their own laughter."

He added: "It had an old-fashioned way-side inn, the Prince of Orange; well we remember it, and its merry-faced and active little landlord, Wiggins, who never would be still, and never could be sad, but with a perennial laugh on his lips and a joke on his tongue, welcomed the weary traveller to cheap and wholesome refreshment. Then there was Mrs. Wiggins who lived in the bar, and of whom nobody ever saw more than the head and shoulders".

It is not clear where Palmer got all his money from. It was presumably inherited, but it is an excellent example of the long term effects of philanthropy. Palmer's original alms house, which merged with several others in 1879 to become the United Westminster Almshouses, is still functioning in Rochester Row, providing sheltered accommodation for 41 men and women over 60 years of age of limited means who have local credentials. The school he founded, known as the Black Coat school - to distinguish it from the Greycoat, Greencoat and Blue Coat schools - eventually joined with others to become today's Westminster City comprehensive in Palace Street.

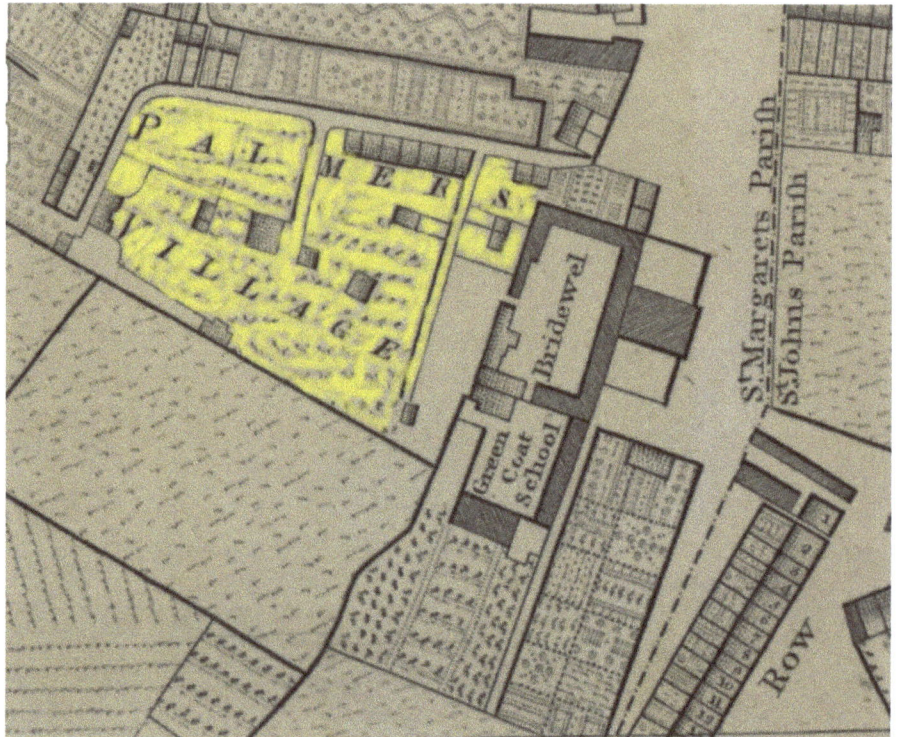

Palmer's Village lasted until Victoria Street blasted its way through the slums in the mid 19th century. On 27th February 1851, the houses were disposed of by auction as part of the so-called Westminster Improvements to make room for the construction of Victoria Street. At the time of writing yet another multi storey, multi purpose edifice is being built on the site of Palmer's Village of a size that could not have been conceived when children were dancing around the maypole in that oasis of Merrie England. I hope the Reverend Palmer is sleeping peacefully.

142

# 49: Thorney Island's influence on the NHS

176  LONDON. — *Westminster Hospital* — LL.

For over 100 years, Thorney Island had its own hospital. It was where the Queen Elizabeth II conference centre is today, facing Westminster Abbey. It was no ordinary hospital. In its time it helped to change the concept of what hospitals were all about. In medieval times, London had had only two big hospitals, Barts and St Thomas's, but they were not really hospitals in the modern sense as their job, believe it or not, wasn't primarily to cure the sick. And for over 400 years there were no new ones.

Medieval hospitals were hostels for beggars, not somewhere you went to be cured. As Rotha Mary Clay (1878 -1961), a historian and social worker pointed out the hospital then was "an ecclesiastical, not a medical institution. It was for care rather than cure; for the relief of the body when possible, but pre-eminently for the refreshment of the soul".

This started to change on 14th January 1716 when rich banker, Henry Hoare, stepped out of the family firm C Hoare and Co in Fleet Street, to St Dunstan's coffee house next door to meet three friends, William Wogan, Robert Witham and a former curate of St Dunstan's church (across the road from Hoare's bank) Patrick Cockburn. They met to discuss a problem no-one else was dealing with: what to do about the scandalous lack of help for the poor sick people of Westminster. Henry volunteered the first donation of £10 for what was to become London's first subscription hospital.

From this unlikely beginning can be traced the birth of Westminster Hospital and later St George's. (Guys came shortly after) Such was the magnitude of the task that it didn't happen instantly. In April of the first year they decided to restrict their efforts to the parish of

St Margaret's, Westminster, "until it shall please God that our stock increases". They presumably chose St Margaret's parish because it was right in the centre of governance serving a growing population of the rich and powerful, but also characterised by extreme poverty and poor living conditions coupled with a paucity of any medical help for the poor.

It was linked to Anglicanism because of Westminster Abbey and St Margaret's church which was almost in the Abbey's back garden. They didn't know that the large hospital they would eventually build would be just across the road from the Abbey.

There followed an unexplained hiatus in their initial activities until December 1718 when a couple of meetings were held including one at Grey Coats school - still on the same site in Greycoat Place today as it was then - when a matron Mrs Jane Alden was appointed at £6 a year.

In 1719, Sir Henry and his founders rented a house in Petty France (then called York Street) to house an infirmary for the needy and in 1720 it opened with only 10 beds, later increased to 20. It was situated across the road from today's Adam and Eve pub at the end of Palmer Street (then called Gardners Lane). It was next door to what later became the site of an international ice rink which staged the World Figure Skating Championships in 1902.

The hospital moved to Chappell Street in 1724 (later renamed Broadway). However, in 1733 there was a serious argument between the Governors and the medical staff as a result of which there was a mass exodus of the medics who migrated to a new site at Hyde Park Corner to found St George's Hospital leaving the governors of the infirmary to pick up the pieces. Which they did by moving to Buckingham Gate (soon to have 91 beds) to be known as the Westminster Infirmary for the Sick. In one sense this was a disaster, but it did lead to another hospital being formed, so Westminster got two hospitals for the price of one.

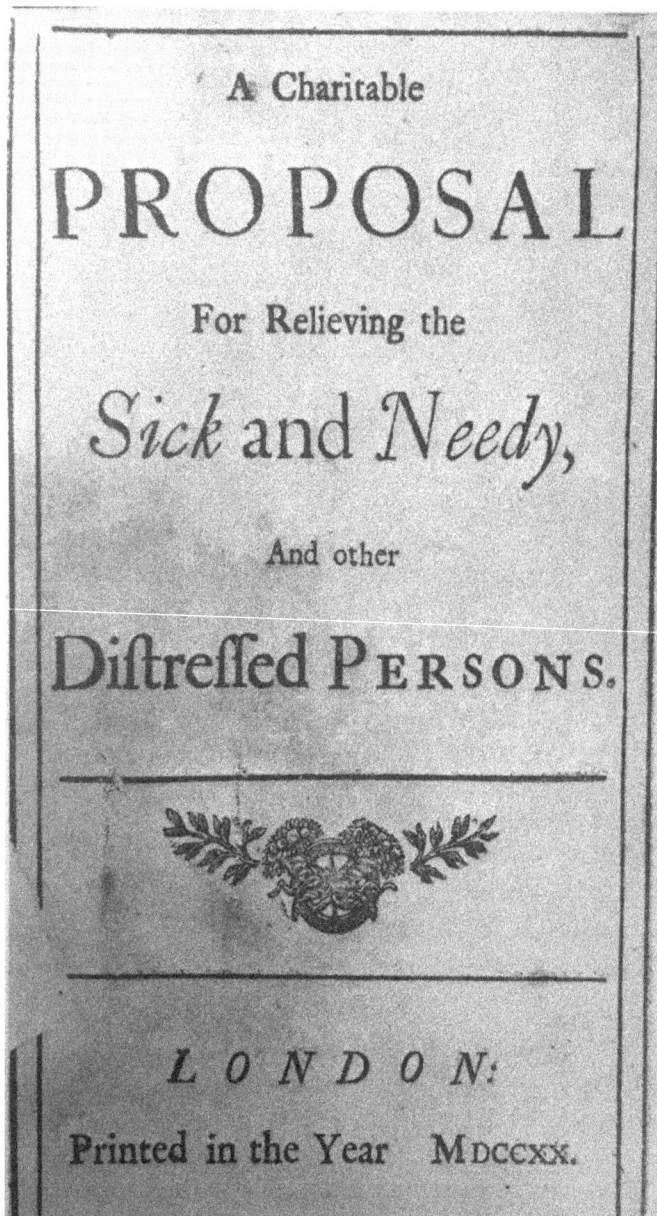

A Charitable

# PROPOSAL

For Relieving the

*Sick* and *Needy,*

And other

Diftreffed PERSONS.

*LONDON:*

Printed in the Year MDCCXX.

The first proposal

*Henry Hoare*

In 1834, a new site opposite Westminster Abbey was purchased from the Treasury which enabled a much bigger hospital to be built in what has been described as "embattled Gothic" style accommodating 200 in-patients or up to 20,000 a year in all. Patients were admitted by permission of one of the governors except for emergency cases who were admitted day or night without recommendation.

In 1938, having lasted over 100 years at the heart of Thorney Island, the Hospital moved yet again. The new building was in St John's Gardens, Westminster (now a block of luxury flats) where it lasted until 1993 when it moved to Fulham Road to become part of the Westminster and Chelsea hospital. It may be difficult for us to believe that hospitals could have existed for over 400 years without having the aim of curing the sick. The new hospital made mistakes on the way - for a long time they declined to treat Roman Catholics - but they were a founding part of a revolution in health care which eventually led to the formation of the National Health Service, much of which happened in and around Thorney Island.

# 50: Roubiliac's statue, a novel made flesh

Louis Roubiliac's monument to Lieutenant General William Hargrave is a Gothic novel made flesh. It glares down on us from a height as if the Heavens have opened to remind us of the resurrection of the General on judgement day as he rises defiantly from his tomb. He shakes off his shroud while the walls of a pyramid are crashing behind him and the bearded angel of Time breaks the lance of a vanquished skeleton of a defeated Death, easing the passage to eternal life.

It must be all too much for visitors passing among the hundreds of sculptures lining the walls of the Abbey to fully absorb it. I wonder how many can see the tiny figure at the top left of an angel sounding the Last Trumpet.

The monument commemorates two people - General Hargrave, who was baptised next door in St Margaret's church, and his friend General Fleming who is buried nearby. Neither of them are classic British heroes. Hargrave would have remained unknown until the genius of Roubiliac gave him a life of his own.

One curious aspect of the sculpture is that there is a small inlaid plaque saying that it preserves the memory of two faithful friends who lost their lives at sea. There is no evidence that this is what happened and it doesn't really matter. It is Roubiliac's masterpiece that has the last word.

# 51: Where is Henry VIII?

No king had more effect on Thorney Island and its surroundings than Henry VIII. When the fire of 1512 badly damaged the medieval Palace of Westminster, which had lasted for 500 years, instead of rebuilding it, Henry pulled it down. He transported the stone - in thousands of cartloads - to help build a new vastly bigger palace occupying most of what we call Whitehall today. He subsequently appropriated St James's Park, The Green Park - both of which he put a wall around - Hyde Park and today's Regent's Park, to create his own private hunting grounds. This was in addition to over 50 palaces and houses he owned or acquired up and down the country, not to mention unleashing the Reformation which changed Westminster Abbey and religion forever and triggered an economic revolution as huge tracts of monastic lands came onto the market.

A man of such doomsday grandeur would obviously need a tomb to remind posterity of his magnificence and to ensure the longevity of the Tudor dynasty. This Henry planned to do on an epic scale and he started at a very early stage in his rule. The main documented evidence of his plans date back to 1518 but he appears to have started planning for a tomb soon after he was crowned in 1509.

No expense was spared and If things had gone according to plan, Henry would have had a tomb like no other. He appropriated Cardinal Wolsey's partially built tomb including its marble base, statues and pillars and planned to add to this some gilded bronze angels, no less than four life sized statues of the King and his favourite subsequent Queen (Jane Seymour). And if that wasn't enough there would be a statue of the King on horseback under a triumphal

*These are three metre tall Angels commissioned by Cardinal Wolsey for his tomb (Now in the Victoria and Albert museum).*

arch, plus 134 brass figures ranging from John the Baptist to St George.

It was self-aggrandisement on a gargantuan scale, projecting an image of unbridled medieval masculinity that bore no relation to the modest successes he made during his brief but expensive invasion of France in 1513.

*Nelson's coffin in St Paul's Cathedral (intended for Henry VIII)*

None of these survived except a few items such as the actual coffin or sarcophagus and its base which, bizarrely, are part of Nelson's Tomb in St Paul's Cathedral.

Despite Henry's lavish plans, his tomb was still unfinished when he died aged 55 in 1547. His children said they would finish the job but, you know how children are, they never got around to it. If you want to get a glimpse of Henry VIII's tomb you won't find it in Westminster Abbey. You will have to go to St George's Chapel in Windsor Castle where there isn't even a tomb, only a modest black marble slab to mark his burial place in the Quire which was added in 1837 by King William IV.

It says: "In a vault beneath this marble slab are deposited the remains of Jane Seymour, Queen of King Henry VIII, 1537. King Henry VIII, 1547. King

Charles I, 1648 and an infant child of Queen Anne. This memorial was placed here by command of King William IV. 1837." May they rest in peace.

# 52: The house that launched 100 million books

On 4th July 1862, a don at Christchurch College Oxford, Charles Dodgson, took three sisters on a boating trip along the river Isis together with his friend, the sub-dean of Westminster Abbey, Rev Robinson Duckworth. When they stopped for tea on a shady bank, one of the sisters, as she later recalled, implored Dodgson to "tell us a story".

The sister was called Alice and she was enthralled by the tales that emerged about a girl, also called Alice, who followed a white rabbit with a waistcoat down a hole into a mystical wonder world. She begged Dodgson, a mathematician at Christchurch, to write them down. The mathematician, later known as Lewis Carroll, did as he was told (the girl was quite forceful and very curious, even at the age of ten). When Dodgson finished the book he gave her the manuscript. It eventually became Alice's Adventures in Wonderland and its successor, Through the Looking Glass, which have sold over 100 million copies world-wide and been translated into 174 languages. It is still selling strongly today. It was the Harry Potter of its day.

pursuit of a white rabbit. At the top of the arch is the eroded coat of Arms of Henry VIII.

Alice returned to the Abbey on 15th September 1880, aged 28 to get married to Reginald Hargreaves – a pupil of Dodgson's at ChristChurch. She was happy to live a private life until 1928, when money problems forced her to sell Dodgson's manuscript to an American collector which triggered something like a national outcry.

Twenty years later, the original manuscript was returned to the UK, in gratitude for Britain fighting with the US in the Second World War. It is now one of the treasured possessions of the British Library and can be viewed online. Alice wasn't buried here, but an article in the Westminster Abbey Review points out that in the quire of the Abbey, Robinson Duckworth, sub dean of the Abbey, is buried. He is assured of a

What is less well-known is a connection between the fictional Alice and the real-life Alice - Alice Liddell - with Thorney Island. She was born in 1852, a year after the opening of Victoria Street, the daughter of Rev Henry George Liddell, the headmaster of Westminster School. She was baptised in the Abbey and lived in the house (picture above) in Dean's Yard Westminster for four years before her parents moved up the Thames to Oxford when her father was appointed Dean of Christchurch. Liddell's arch is the main entrance to Little Dean's Yard, the centre of the school, and it is easy to imagine Alice scampering through the arch in

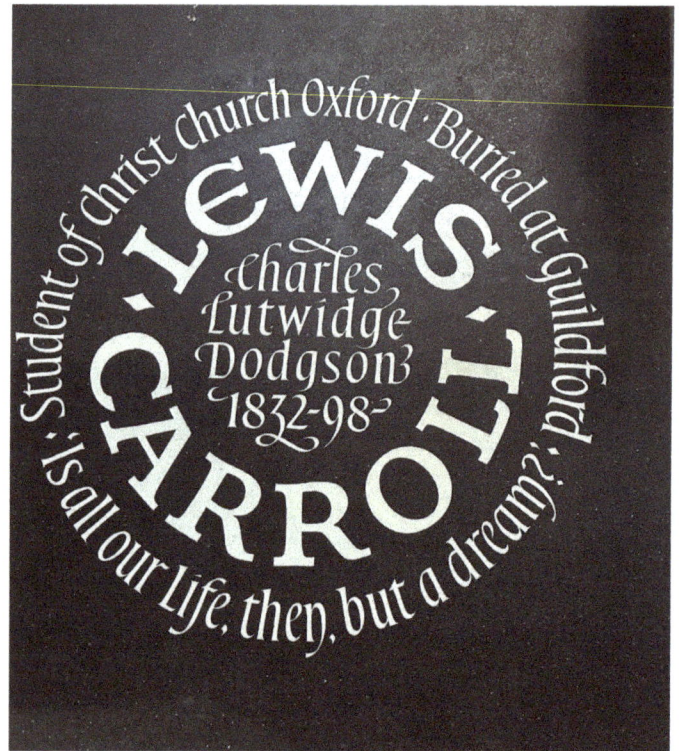

Student of Christ Church Oxford · Buried at Guildford · 'Is all our Life, then, but a dream?'. LEWIS · CARROLL · Charles Lutwidge Dodgson 1832-98

*Duckworth, a distinguished figure in the history of the Abbey, also has a small stained glass window along the way to the Little Cloister depicting St Francis in a wonderland of his own amid birds of all kinds.*

small but fascinating place in literary history. He was rowing the boat at the time the tale was told by Lewis Carroll and is memorialised in the book, with a riff on his name. He is the Duck in the Jury Box and the Duck in the Pool of Tears. His grave is marked by a dotted line in the Abbey's Quire near where he used to sit. It is unusual to have a dotted line to mark your grave. It's the sort of dotty thing that might have happened in Wonderland.

There is one more link in what might one day become a themed Wonderland journey for visitors. Neither Alice nor Carroll were buried in the Abbey, but in 1982 a memorial stone to Carroll was unveiled at Poets Corner. Unlike the surrounding stones - for Byron, D H Larence, Henry James, Dylan Thomas and T S Eliot, that of Lewis Carroll is round. Clearly a rabbit hole waiting for another iconic visitor.

# 53: The man who saved Britain's early history

From this house sprung the richest private collection of books and manuscripts ever recorded in the UK. It exceeded the collections of the Royal Library, the Inns of Court and the College of Arms. They were collected by Sir Robert Bruce Cotton MP (1571–1631) whose house, the ruins of which along with other debris are shown in this illustration, was situated between the Painted Chamber and the Thames in Old Palace Yard. It became the meeting-place of many of the eminent scholars of England, including Francis Bacon, Ben Jonson, Inigo Jones, Sir Walter Raleigh and Lord Salisbury. Cotton lived with his collection in this house from 1622 until his death nine years later. The rough stones in the engraving were apparently the result of the reconstruction of the House of Commons.

Cotton had close connections with Thorney island. He had been educated at Westminster School and was an MP at Westminster for 28 years for various constituencies including the "rotten borough" of Old Sarum.

The Library was eventually given to the nation by Cotton's grandson and was the most prestigious founding donation to what became the British Library.

It could so easily not have happened but for Cotton's bull-nosed determination to make sure that vital historic documents were preserved for the nation.

This was a time, after the Dissolution of the Monasteries, when government documents and priceless historical

*Cotton's house in a dilapidated state. Drawn by J T Smith*

manuscripts regularly fell into the hands of people ignorant of their historic value. History was being unwittingly destroyed. There were even examples of ordinary folk innocently filling bungholes with medieval manuscripts.

Cotton made it his duty and pleasure to buy and preserve them for the nation.

His claim on our gratitude is partly because of the priceless manuscripts he rescued from oblivion - such as the Lindisfarne Gospels, the only copy of Beowulf, two copies of the original Magna Carta, Sir Gavin and the Green Knight and so on.

It is a sobering thought that without that impulsive action we may not have had Tolkien's Lord of the Rings or C S Lewis' Chronicles of Narnia, both of which were inspired by Beowulf. The book continues to be influential today. Seamus Heaney, the great Irish poet, has been much praised for his translation of Beowulf, which was published in 1999 and remains popular today.

*Bust of Robert Bruce Cotton (1571-1631), by Louis-François Roubiliac (1702-1762), (Source Wikipedia and the British Museum)*

We should also be grateful to Cotton because at a time when most libraries were private he allowed others to use them including scholars, politicians and lawyers. It is tempting to think that Shakespeare could have had access to them as he would have overlapped with Sir Robert in the early part of his life. There is, however, no evidence that they knew each other - though they could have.

Cotton was a friend of Ben Jonson and others who were friends of Shakespeare and if Shakespeare did know him he would have had potential access to his library which might help to explain where part of Shakespeare's vast knowledge came from. Cotton was also a member of the fraternity of the Mermaid Tavern off Cheapside which is also believed to have counted Shakespeare as a member. The landlord of the Mermaid, William Johnson, was listed as a trustee for the mortgage when Shakespeare purchased the Blackfriars gatehouse in March 1613, so they must have known each other very well.

From 1603, for a period, Cotton lived in the small enclave of Blackfriars where Shakespeare's troupe, the Lord Chamberlain's Men, had purchased a theatre in 1596 even though they were not allowed to move in to use it until 1609. It is difficult to believe they didn't come across each other, but like so many other things about Shakespeare's life there is no proof.

Whatever else, that collection, according to the historian Kevin Sharpe, was "a library of manuscripts, possessing a monopoly of the most important material for early English history". An introduction to the Act of Parliament establishing trusts for the Cottonian Library said it was "generally esteemed the best collection of its kind now anywhere extant."

Cotton certainly took care of it. He had it organised according to the exact position of each book in a room that was 26 feet long and six feet wide. For instance

"Vitellius A.xv" meant under the bust of Vitellius on the top shelf (A), count fifteen (xv) across for the volume which included the only surviving manuscript of Beowulf. The manuscripts are, apparently, still catalogued in this way in the British Library.

The Cotton collection was not only highly valuable but because it was also fairly freely available, highly controversial. Information, or data, in those days, as now, was powerful and the Government didn't want it to get into the wrong hands.

In 1629, Cotton was arrested for making available a pamphlet held to be seditious. As it turned out, it had actually been written earlier by someone else.

He was released, but it didn't stop the library being closed on this pretext. It remained closed until after his death and was not restored to his son and heir, Sir Thomas Cotton, until 1633.

Long after Cotton's death, Charles I stayed at the house, which was still owned by his family, during his trial. It commenced in January 1649, when the High Court met in the Painted Chamber a few yards away from Cotton's residence to convict Charles for treason. His death warrant was most likely signed in the Painted Chamber before the court moved a few days later to Westminster Hall close by which had been fitted up, in every sense, for the King's trial.

Over the years the library was located in several places, most notably Essex House in the Strand from 1712 to 1730. It then made an ill-fated move in 1731 to Ashburnham House (now part of Westminster School). The following year fire destroyed some of the most important parts of the collection.

Thirteen manuscripts were lost and over 200 others suffered severe destruction and water damage. The librarian, Dr. Bentley escaped from the fire while clutching under one arm the priceless Codex Alexandrinus which contains most of the Greek Old and New Testaments. One of the worst losses was a unique manuscript of the Life of King Alfred the Great.

Sir Robert's grandson, Sir John Cotton, donated the library to Great Britain upon his death in 1702. In 1753, the library was transferred to the new British Museum, under the Act of Parliament which established it. The Act stated that the library was to 'be kept and preserved ... "for Publick Use and Advantage", and that it should "not be sold, or otherwise disposed of".

At the same time the Sloane Collection, donated by Sir Hans Sloane and the Harley Collection by Edward Harley, the Earl of Oxford were acquired. These three became the museum's "foundation collections". The Royal manuscripts were donated by George II in 1757 and in 1973 all became part of the newly established British Library. The soul of the library is still the foundation volumes so many of which were saved from oblivion by Sir Robert. It could so easily not have been so.

# 54: The perils of marrying for money

"Ah! sure such a pair was never seen so justly form'd to meet by nature" *to shew* Dedicated to Old Bags

Every monarch since William the Conqueror has been crowned at Westminster Abbey, but none quite like George IV. Some royal marriages are made in Heaven. Others in another place. Regarding that of George IV and Princess Caroline of Brunswick in 1795, readers must decide for themselves. For George it was love at first sight…

…of the money involved. Before his marriage, the profligate lifestyle of the Prince of Wales had racked up debts of £600,000 from gambling and extravagant living which weighed in at an astonishing - and difficult

to believe - £92 million in today's money. He needed anything he could get.

Parliament helped to bail him out by offering £65,000 a year (worth millions in today's money), plus a possible extra £100,000 to reduce his debts, but only on the condition that he agreed to a political marriage to his cousin Caroline of Brunswick, whose dowry was a comparatively modest £50,000 in old money. In other words, Parliament was bribing George with £65,000 a year to marry a suitable Protestant bride.

George succumbed and the marriage ceremony was conducted in the Chapel Royal in St James's Palace on the evening of 8th April 1795. Caroline turned up in an elegant white gown with a coronet. George turned up drunk and boisterous and avoided his bride during the ceremony.

They had a child together, Charlotte, and that was the end of their relationship though his efforts to divorce her were thwarted by Parliament as was his earlier attempt in 1785 to illegally marry Mrs Fitzherbert.

George was determined to avoid a scene like this happening again at his coronation twenty-six years later in 1821. There was only one way. He decided to ban his wife from attending his coronation ceremony.

He insisted that no one should be admitted without a ticket, and he made sure that she wasn't issued with a ticket. This didn't stop Caroline from trying on several occasions to gain entry, but despite initial support from the crowd their enthusiasm eventually waned.

George survived the lavish banquet in a state that was not recorded. The problem was how would he get home? His normal route up Whitehall into the Mall and then to Carlton

House was too crowded with people for the carriages to get through. Opinions differ as to whether, as some warned, his safety might be at risk because of unfriendly crowds or, more likely there were just too many onlookers around trying to be part of the coronation ceremony.

Whatever the reason, it was decided that the King had to go home by a different route. This meant travelling down Abingdon Street and Millbank through Five Fields, a circuitous route to the back entrance to

*Coronation Banquet of George IV in Westminster Hall, 1821 (Parliamentary Art Collection)*

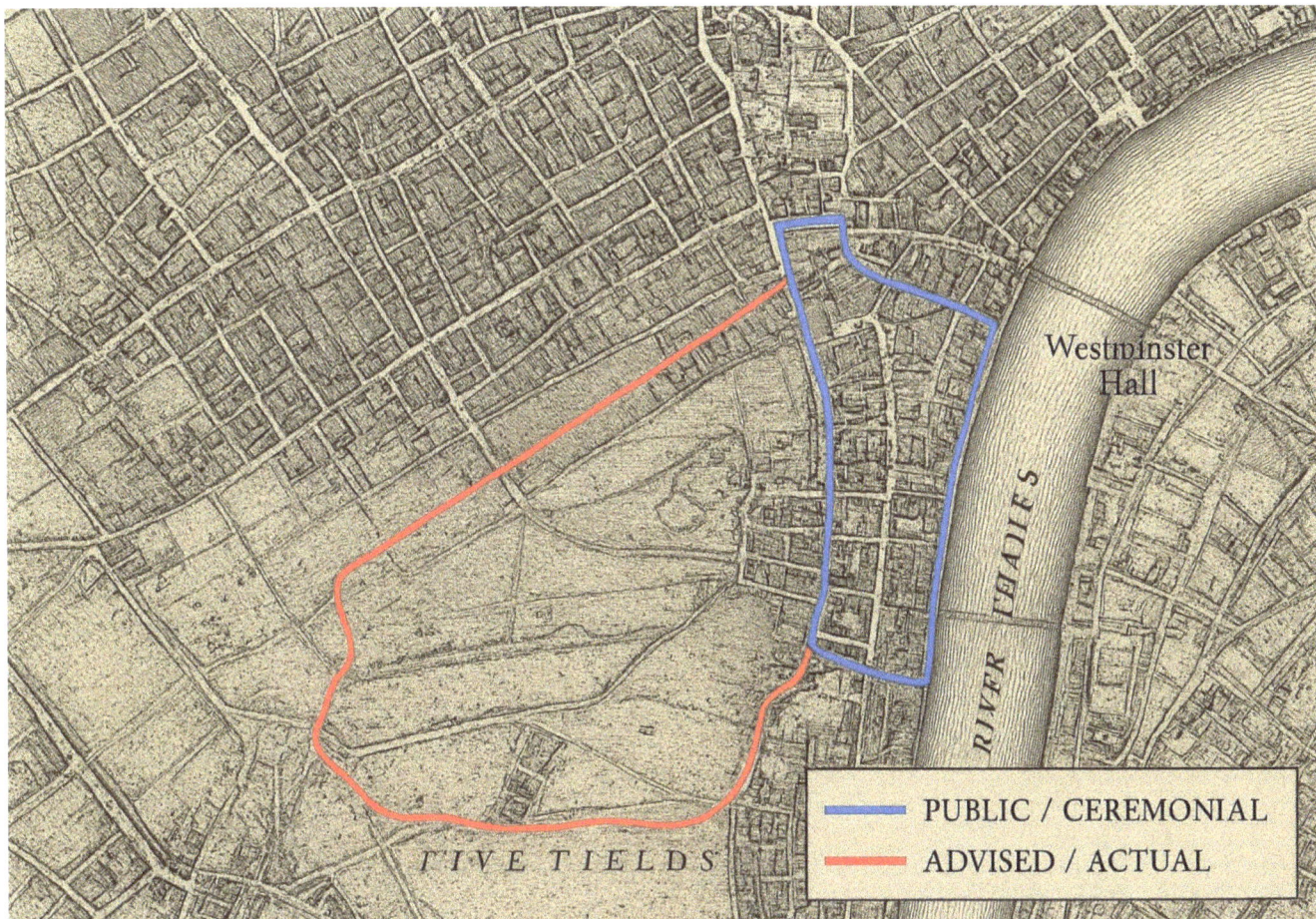

*How George got home after the coronation banquet (in red) Thanks, ChatGPT*

Carlton House. To the King must have seemed like bandit country.

After all that, it is no great surprise that George IV was not one of our most successful Kings. He was a significant patron of the arts, and he didn't involve the country in any foreign wars, but his continued extravagance and loose living made him unpopular among taxpayers.

There were plans to place a bronze statue of him on top of the Marble Arch at a time when the Arch itself was going to be outside Buckingham Palace, but that was found to be badly positioned for a passage into the Palace. Instead, a temporary resting place was found on a plinth in Trafalgar Square where it can still be viewed, presumably, still temporarily.

George didn't have any luck with bridges either. Vauxhall Bridge, which he must have passed close to on his way back from his coronation, was originally named Regent Bridge when he was Prince Regent before becoming King. It was shortly afterward renamed Vauxhall Bridge to attract more visitors to the fashionable Vauxhall Gardens.

# 55: The lethal legacy of Tothill Fields

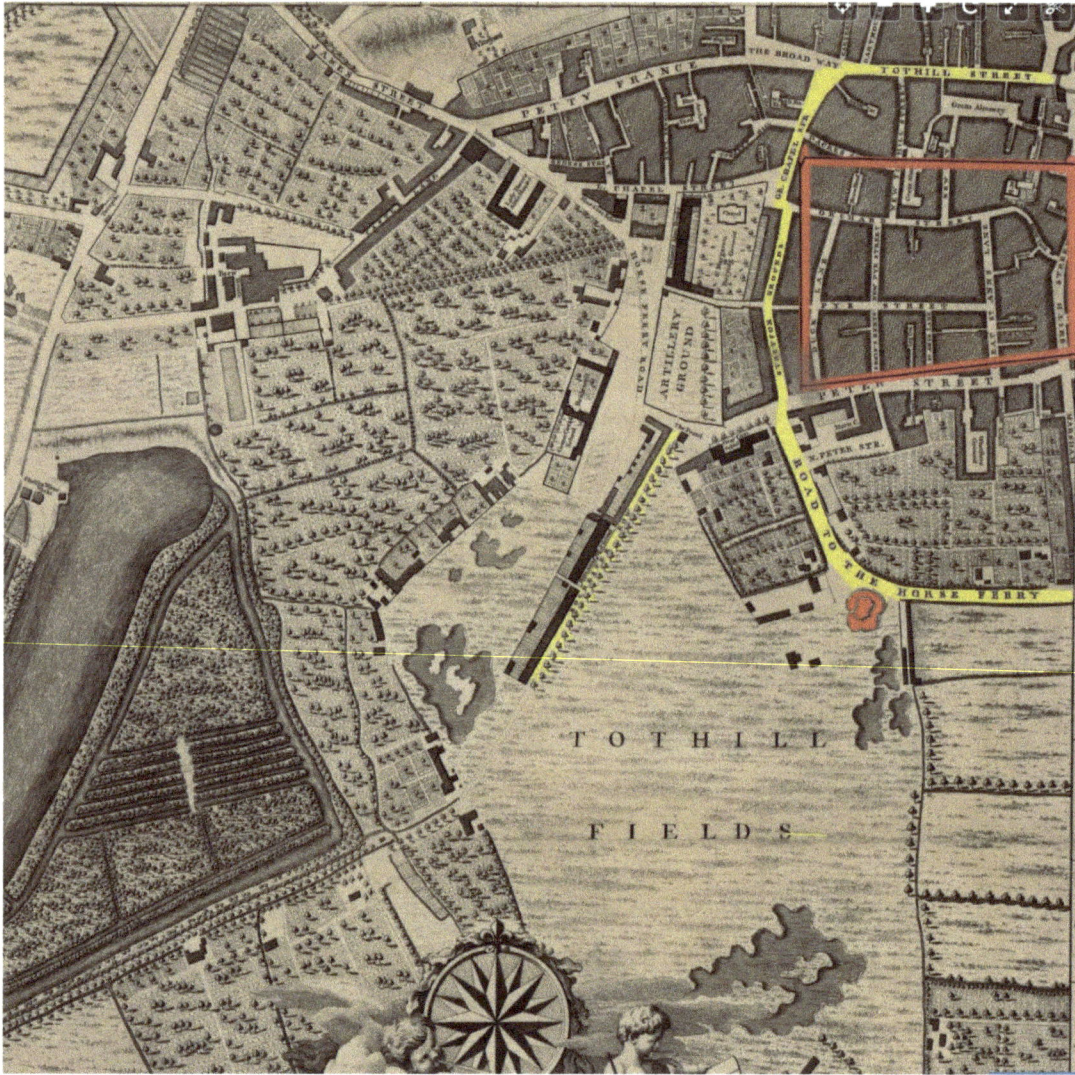

John Rocque's map (c1746) shows (in yellow) the road from Tothill Street to Horseferry Road on the way to the Thames at today's Lambeth Bridge. The "Toot" or raised look-out mound which gave rise to its name is coloured red on the turn of Horseferry Road. Rochester Row is in thin yellow on the left and the notorious "Devil's Acre", arguably the most deprived and criminalised area in the whole country, is marked within the red square on the right.

Thorney Island can't be put into context without mentioning Tothill Fields which hems it in on its western side just as the Thames does on the east. It dates back at least as far as 1236 when it hosted tournaments and jousts. It gave its name to Tothill Street, one of the oldest thoroughfares in old Westminster, which is the entrance to the core of Thorney Island at the top of the map. The street joins Stretton (Strutton) Ground and then

Horseferry Road on the way to the Thames. It provides a protective ring around the roads of old Westminster before the wild west of Tothill Fields begins. The thin yellow line on the left of Tothill Fields flanked by tiny trees in the map above is Rochester Row, for centuries a private lane to the country retreat of the Abbots of Westminster Abbey at Neyte in Chelsea.

The most flamboyant event to be staged on Tothill Fields was as far back as 1256, when John Mansell, the King's councillor and also a rich priest, hosted the dinner to end all dinners. It was too large to be held at his house in Tothill Street so he set up tents and pavilions in the wilderness of Tothill Fields. The A-list guests included King Richard III and Queen Eleanor of Provence, the King and Queen of Scotland and a dizzy array of barons and knights.

The scale of the event is reflected in the fact that "seven hundred messes of meat did not serve for the first dinner". It was so big that it was wrongly thought to have been a Coronation feast for Richard and Eleanor. Mansell is remembered today by Maunsell Street off Vincent Square.

After that it was all ups and downs. There was a bright side to Tothill Fields, but also a tragic one. John Strype (1643-1737) said that the fields were noted "for supplying London and Westminster with asparagus, artichokes, cauliflowers and musk melons" but the 17th century had a darker shadow when Tothill Fields

*Painting by G Arnald, 1807*

159

VIEW of the PEST-HOUSES at TOTHILL FIELDS.

*Published Aug. 6, 1796 by I. Stockdale, Piccadilly*

*The Pest Houses by Edward Dayes*

became more like the Killing Fields when it was used as the makeshift burial ground during plagues and the scene of a military catastrophe.

It is reckoned that during the plague of 1665 an astonishing 3,000 bodies were buried at the expense of the Parish. Samuel Pepys wrote in his diary of 16th October 1665: "They tell me that in Westminster there is never a physician and but one apothecary left, all being dead". Pepys complained that the cemetery of New Chapel Yard had been walled off and only the rich could afford to be interred there, the rest being buried in the open fields and covered with thick layers of soil.

Tothill Fields was formerly known as Bulinga Fen, a

160

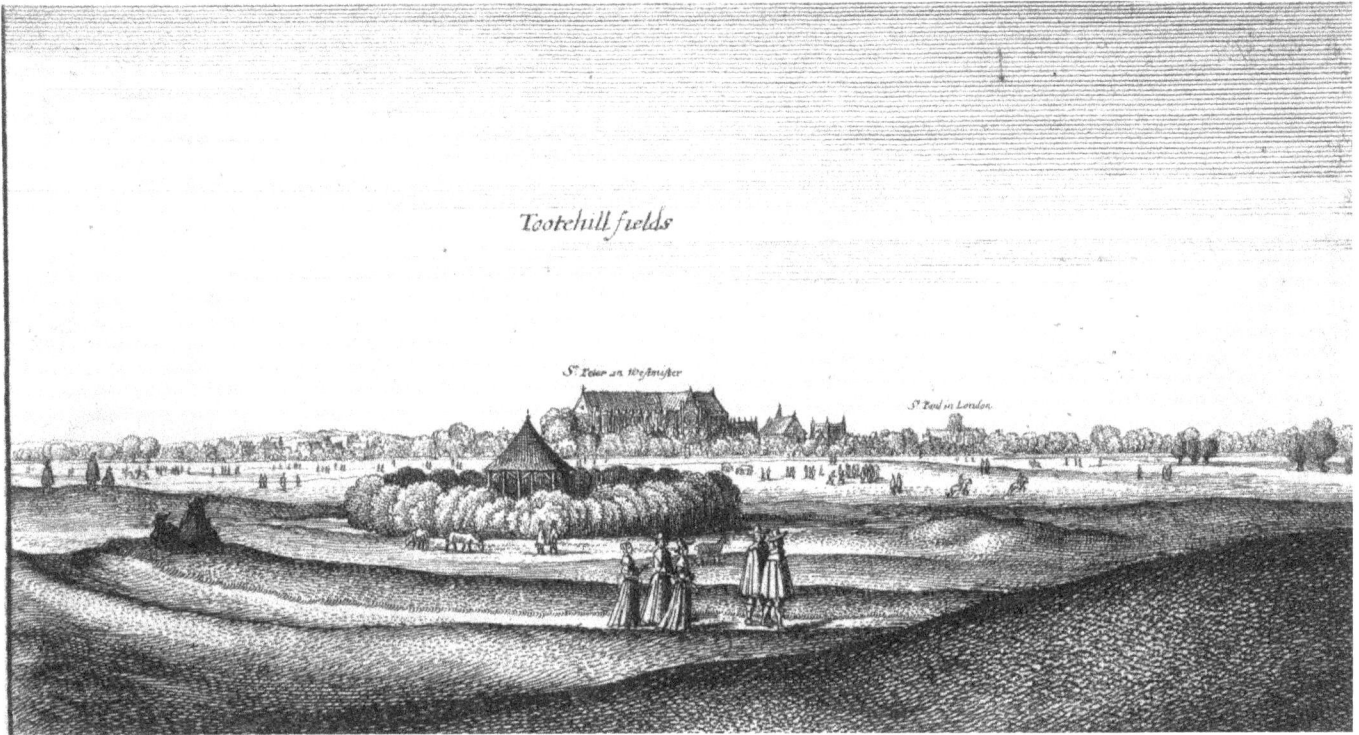

*Tothill Fields by Wenceslaus Hollar (1607 - 1677)*

marshy, frequently flooded, swamp which followed the river along Millbank (where there is still a road called Bulinga Street behind Tate Britain) until it drained away leaving what J E Smith called "a tract of peaty soil afterwards known as Tothill-Fields."

Around 960 A.D., Saint Dunstan, who was then Bishop of London, established a monastery on the site of "ruined chapels" located in the marshland of Thorn Ea, at Bulinga Fen. It was the perfect place for a contemplative existence, being two miles from the city of London and with hardly any habitation in Bulinga Fen. The picture (above) by G Arnald was painted in 1807. It shows how little had changed by then, barely three years before William Vincent, Dean of Westminster, carved out part of Tothill Fields for the playing fields of Westminster School in what is now

known as Vincent Square (though it is actually shaped like a diamond not a square).

With a certain amount of artistic licence - the area was much more built up by 1807 than the painting suggests - it shows a view of the Abbey from Rochester Row where the trees can be seen. A horse and cart in the middle distance is meandering its way along Horseferry Road (formerly Market Street) towards the horse ferry by the river. In between is the start of Tothill Fields.

Over the centuries, Tothill Fields has witnessed all human life as it evolved from a swampy wasteland and the haunt of highwaymen, to a playground for school children and an emerging market garden with prize asparagus and melons.

Before the 15th century, it was a mustering ground for

troops who had to be proficient with England's battle-winning adoption of the longbow which helped to secure victory at Crecy during the Hundred Years War in 1346. In the 16th and 17th century, wrestling, cock fighting and a primitive form of football took over. During the 17th century it was the scene of military training and the burial of bodies during outbreaks of plague.

J E Smith, the Vestry clerk for the parishes of St Margaret, and St John the Evangelist in his book "Parochial Memorials", writes about cock fighting and bear baiting including this advertisement from the reign of Queen Anne about a famous bear garden in Tothill Fields "upon part of the site of Vincent Square". "At William Well's Bear Garden in Tothill Fields, this present Monday, the 10th of April (1703) will be a green bull baited, and twenty doggs fight for a collar… with other versions of bull-baiting and bear baiting. Beginning at two of the clock."

The memory of Tothill Fields that haunts the place to this day brought humanity to a new low. After Oliver Cromwell's victory at the Battle of Worcester in 1651, which ended the Civil War, thousands of defeated Scottish soldiers were marched in sub-human conditions from the battlefield at Worcester to Tothill Fields where an estimated 1,200 of them died from disease, starvation or maltreatment en route or were executed when they arrived. The "lucky" ones escaped death only to be sold as white slaves to merchants operating in Guinea or the Caribbean.

There were far too many bodies to be buried in the cemetery of New Chapel, the chapel of ease for St Margaret's Church where Christchurch Gardens in Victoria Street is today. Instead the corpses were buried in mass graves in Tothill Fields, which almost certainly included part of the land that is today's Vincent Square.

A permanent 'pest-house' known as "The Sheds" was established by Lord Craven as a lazaretto or isolation hospital for victims of the Great Plague when Tothill Fields became a burial ground for the dead when graveyards overflowed. It became a feared place as the ground could not be consecrated under church law.

In the 17th century, people used to resort to a "Maze" in these same fields, which, according to a contemporary writer, was much frequented in the summer-time, the fields being described as "of great use, pleasure, and recreation," to the King's Scholars of Westminster School and neighbours.

Hollar's engraving gives a romanticised view of Tothill Fields with well-dressed visitors in the foreground and a maze in the middle, but among the small figures huddled at the back it looks as though a duel was taking place. It is possible that the mound, bottom right, could be all, or part, of the raised look-out that gave rise to the word Toot-hill.

Today nothing remains to remind residents and visitors of Tothill Fields except the name of a road. The names "Tute" or Toot or Toot-hill referred long ago to a raised look-out post which is known to have existed as recently as 1804 when the parish Vestry was granted permission to convey "the rubbish in the hill in Tothill Fields" to raise the level of a nearby burial ground. The hill or mound is commonly thought to have been on the curve of Horseferry Road - where the red-coloured blob is on the Roque map above. It is perhaps worth a thought as you zoom past in your car. Or maybe even a toot.

# 56: Edward the Confessor: the good and the not so good

It is impossible to write about Thorney Island without mentioning (St) Edward the Confessor. Without him there may never have been a Westminster Abbey as we know it. He was born around 1003 in Oxfordshire, the son of a French mother, Emma of Normandy and King Ethelred the Unready (meaning poorly advised) of Wessex. He was driven into exile to Normandy by the Danes. Edward apparently vowed that if he returned safely to England he would make a pilgrimage to Rome. He didn't make that pilgrimage, but was released from his vow by the Pope on condition that he would re-found a monastery for St Peter. This led to him to build a new church at Westminster which he largely financed by himself from his royal revenues and gifts from the nobles. These days we might call it a sovereign wealth fund.

Shrine of (St) Edward the Confessor

The Abbey was later reconstructed in the Gothic style by Henry III in the 13th century to become the Abbey we know today. Henry was greatly influenced by Edward's piety and the attraction of his tomb in the Abbey which had become a place of pilgrimage.

Edward was known as the Confessor though there is no evidence that he ever went to confession to a priest (unlike future kings such as Richard II and Henry V, who did). His piety was not in question, but his failure to produce an heir and his disproportionate reliance on noble families such as the Godwins had lasting political consequences for England. Not to put too fine a point on it, if he had produced a successor it would almost certainly have undermined William the Conqueror's claim to the throne and the horrendous consequences of his eventual success.

The cult of St Edward was greatly fashioned by the determination of Osbert de Clare, Prior of Westminster, long after Edward's death, to have him canonised. Osbert was a sort of ecclesiastical spin doctor who wrote a hagiography of Edward and campaigned in Rome for his canonisation, portraying him as a holy man and worker of claimed, but not proven, miracles. After initial failures, Edward was eventually canonised in 1161 by Pope Alexander III, a few years after de Clares's death. However, canonisation didn't lead to Edward becoming the Patron Saint of England.

In 1350, another Edward - King Edward III - chose an early Christian martyr, St George, as the Patron Saint of England when he formed the Order of the Garter, even though there was no evidence that George ever visited England. However, his status as a warrior martyr was more in keeping with the spirit of the times as endorsed by the battle cry of Shakespeare's Henry V: "Cry Go for Harry, England and St George".

The Confessor may have failed to become England's Patron Saint, but his Abbey, which has crowned every king since William the Conqueror, has become a prime national memory and a huge attraction for tourists, especially from overseas. England may no longer be the political force it once was, but exploiting the legacy of its past has become a new source of economic growth.

*Edward the Confessor from the Bayeux Tapestry*

# Lost London 1

This is the map from the first Lost London book, which is available from most online retailers, or you can get a discounted copy from the author, if you can collect from central London.

Contact Vic Keegan - victor.keegan@gmail.com

# Lost London 2

This is the map from the second Lost London book, which is available from most online retailers, or you can get a discounted copy from the author, if you can collect from central London.

Contact Vic Keegan - victor.keegan@gmail.com

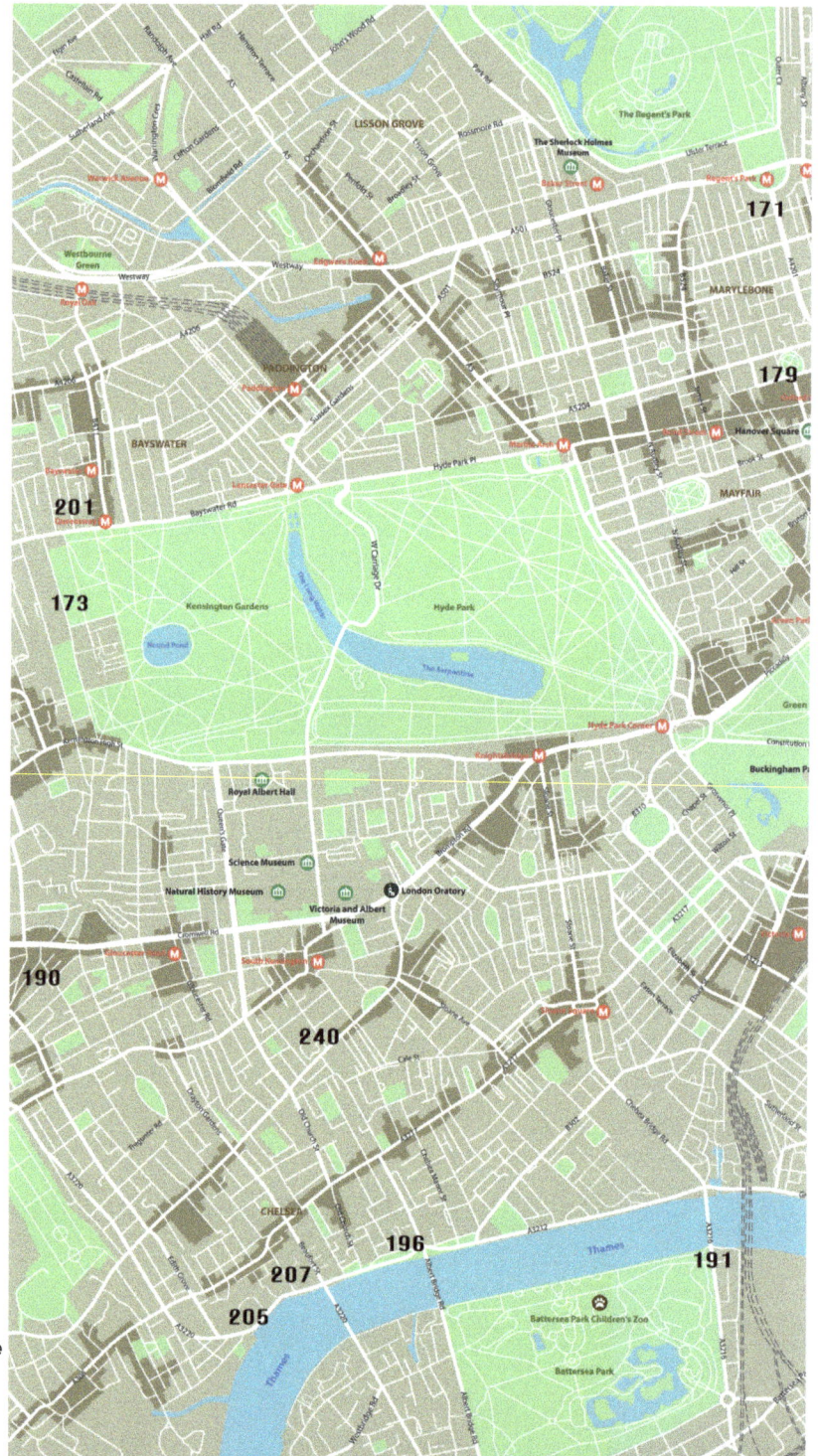

*Numbers are placed in approximate places. Those on the very edge indicate locations off the map.*

207  197  193

214
SAINT PANCRAS
210
178
225
219
171
262 264
261 260
254 257
GOLDEN
LANE ESTATE
195
258 242 252 265
Russell Square
247 167
259 251 250 245
The British Museum
263 165 256 243
249 Museum of London
202 244 266 253 Lincoln's Inn Fields 182
179 248 246 Hunterian Museum 276
216 255 Royal Courts of Justice 206 215 270 286 273
MAYFAIR 212 Temple Church 224 203 283 285 272 280
177 231 172 161 200 Temple Church 164 277 282
183 234 St Paul's Cathedral 227 274
National Portrait Gallery 232 239 235 Blackfriars Bridge Millennium Bridge 284 275 271
237 St Martin-in-the-Fields 278 170
192 162 220 199 211 National Theatre 160 185 Monument to the Great Fire of London 194
238 222 174 187 279
209 236 London Eye Southwark Cathedral 189
Buckingham Palace 184 Westminster Bridge 184 163
223 186 176 Big Ben 169 230 Tower Bridge
228 218 198 217 Palace of Westminster 175 City Hall
229 226 Westminster Abbey
Westminster Cathedral 168 213 Imperial War Museum 281
208
NEWINGTON
WALWORTH
241

# About the Author

Victor Keegan, a born and bred Londoner, claims to have been doing exactly the same job every day of his working life: that is rearranging the 26 letters of the alphabet into different combinations while trying to avoid saying the same thing twice. It started when he was involved with two joint Cambridge and Oxford magazines, *Cameo* and *Image*, with his brother William (who still writes a regular economics column for *The Observer* after nearly 50 years)

It gathered pace when he joined *The Guardian* reporting about news, finance, economics, the internet, virtual worlds and mobile phones. He had a fortnightly column on economics and industry for nearly 25 years, followed by a weekly column on the digital revolution. His most satisfying creative time was launching the first text message poetry competition on *The Guardian* with colleagues.

In retirement, he started writing poems and has so far written six books on a large range of subjects from the future of the universe to a nun on the London Underground. He was a sort of poet in residence at the wonderful Illuminate Rotherhithe event in 2019 and the When the Oak Spoke festival at Wadhurst in Kent, also in 2019, plus the London Urban Forest Festival.

Poetry carried on until he fell in love...

...with London. He had lived there most of his life, but it was only years after he had moved with his family to Victoria that he became entranced by the history beneath his feet. He was amazed to find that within walking distance of their apartment there had been three large prisons, the biggest and most prestigious piano manufacturer in the world and next to where Westminster Tube station is today what was claimed to be the grandest opera house in Europe was built up to roof level before the money ran out and it had to be dismantled. Further research revealed hundreds of other examples which resulted in Vic Keegan's Lost London (1) and Vic Keegan's Lost London 2 and now this book on Thorney Island.

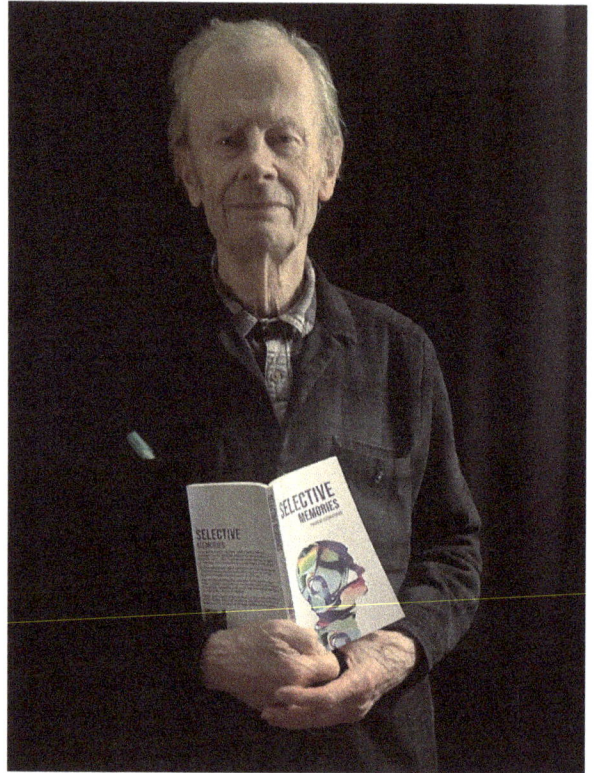

# Acknowledgements

More books have probably been written about the small area covered by Thorney Island than anywhere else in Britain. This is no surprise since these few acres have been host to Westminster Abbey, two Houses of Parliament, Westminster School, a Sanctuary full of criminals and for over 500 years practically all the law courts and the Royal Palace from where the whole country was ruled.

My thanks must go to the dozens and dozens of books I have dipped into, an increasing number of which are now online.

Two books of recent origin stand out:

*WESTMINSTER*

The Art, Architecture, and Archaeology of the Royal Abbey and Palace.

Edited by Warwick Rodwell and Tim Tatton-Brown

*WESTMINSTER II*

The Art, Architecture, and Archaeology of the Royal Palace.

Edited by Warwick Rodwell and Tim Tatton-Brown

I am very grateful to Dr Matthew Payne, Keeper of the Muniments at Westminster Abbey and Christine Reynolds, Assistant Keeper for their invaluable assistance, and to Dr Mark Collins, Estates Historian & Archivist at the Houses of Parliament, to Jan Pancheri, former head gardener at the Abbey, Elizabeth Biggs, Dr Elizabeth Wells, Archivist at Westminster School and Penny Swan, Librarian at The Grey Coat Hospital school.

Also, Tim Tatton Brown, the distinguished archaeological consultant, Stephen Foster, Mary Nicholls, Head of Environmental Archaeology at Museum of London Archaeology (Mola) for its unrivalled knowledge of the history of the island.

Many thanks to Westminster Archives, in St Ann's Street, a treasure trove of information about the history of the whole of Westminster. I am deeply indebted to their ever friendly staff past and present. Thanks also to Patterson Joseph, the actor, who brought the life of Ignatius Sancho, the black polymath, to life in the church of St Margaret's where he was married and encouraged me to continue writing when my energy was flagging.

As always there must be special thanks to Wikipedia, an oasis of calm, preserving the ethos of the original internet before it was colonised by corporations. I hope it survives the onslaught of the new AI search engines which have given a fresh dimension to search with as yet little known long-term consequences.

www.ingramcontent.com/pod-product-compliance
Lightning Source LLC
Chambersburg PA
CBHW040246100426
42811CB00011B/1174